A
Formula
of
His
Own

John J. Conder

A Formula of His Own

Henry Adams's
Literary
Experiment

The University
of Chicago Press

Chicago and London

Standard Book Number: 226–11437–6
Library of Congress Catalog Card Number: 79–103427

The University of Chicago Press, Chicago 60637
The University of Chicago Press, Ltd., London

© 1970 by The University of Chicago
All rights reserved. Published 1970
Printed in the United States of America

To my wife
Barbara McCamus Conder

Contents

Preface

No one today challenges the judgment that *Mont-Saint-Michel and Chartres* and Henry Adams's *Education* are, to put it simply, works of art. In this sense criticism of two books which Adams thought of as a single unit, "the one . . . meaningless without the other," has leaped a giant step past earlier opinions slighting the *Chartres* for inaccurate history and the *Education* for morbidness. But given its many merits, a substantial body of criticism still has not established that direct relation between book and audience of which Adams despaired when he wrote privately that "not one reader in a thousand ever understands," or when he commented in a prefatory note to the *Chartres*, "The relationship between reader and writer, of son and father, may have existed in Queen Elizabeth's time, but is much too close to be true for ours." Of course, for Adams denial was always a form of provocation, in this case an invitation to the reader to try to make contact; and so, in his usual sardonic fashion, he segmented his audience, addressing the *Chartres* to nieces, the *Education* to young men. Perhaps he could antagonize men into understanding the *Chartres* and seduce young ladies into the pages of the *Education*.

Their methods may be different, but the critic and the artist must share the same goals, with the critic supplementing the work of art by *re*establishing and *re*enforcing that confrontation between reader and writer which Adams, demurrers notwithstanding, so genuinely desired. If criticism of Adams's late works has been inhibited in this its chief function, it is due largely to the approaches it has adopted. Full length studies have diluted the individuality of the books, not treating them as the experiments in literary form which Adams repeatedly called them but submerging them in some intellectual or literary "figure in the carpet" which the critic has perceived running throughout all Adams's works. Within a scheme of Adams's drift from eighteenth-century confidence to twentieth-century nihilism, or from an ordered universe to a supersensual chaos, the distinct qualities which separate the *Chartres* and the *Education* from earlier works obviously different in form are all but lost. Such schemes have their value, and this study begins by applying one briefly to Adams's major works; but it is done to emphasize the literary uniqueness of his masterpieces, not simply the continuity of his thought.

A second reason for the failure of a direct confrontation with the books has to do with Adams's professed intentions. He called the works literary experiments, but he added scientific and didactic motives to boot; and for the most part critics have ignored or denied the relevance of the extra-literary motives, again losing a good deal of their unique quality. This study asks whether these motives do exist and, if so, whether they coexist successfully to create a special literary experiment. These are the questions I propose to answer in the following chapters, being fully aware of the problems involved. There is the problem of Adams's calling the books a unit, although it seems likely that he did not plan the *Education* as he began to write the earlier *Chartres*. There is the problem of his linking both books with scientific essays written later, although one aspect of his later scientific interest, entropy, was not in his mind during their composition. And finally, there is the problem of how the presumed scientific and didactic intentions combine with the literary motive he prized so highly.

I try to eliminate these problems by showing what I believe to be the proper relation among all these motives. This sets the stage for the larger part of my study. By demonstrating how the extraliterary motives point to special literary methods used in the books, I try to establish those techniques which give the books their own special individuality independent of Adams's other work, and to suggest the levels of meaning implied by these strategies. Although I recognize important symbols in each work—I hardly need mention the Virgin and the dynamo—I find that neither depends upon symbols to achieve that unity of form to which Adams passionately committed himself and which he thought had failed toward the end of the *Education*. One critic called the *Education* "the story of objects rising into symbols through the perspective of years." But in books composed of hundreds of objects, events, figures, and observations—all symbolic—it seems unlikely that individual symbols alone structure a narrative and it is probable that some other control governs to establish unity of form. And so, in searching for this intended unity, I found the various elements of historical and personal experience united by a fictional persona and by recurrent methods of presenting material in a widely varying, often sharply opposed, set of contexts. Through this repetition of method in radically different circumstances, Adams created a unified structure as well as a dynamic kind of tension between an apparently free narrator and a world of more powerful forces.

My emphasis is on technique, but I seek no abstruse or comfortable little system which "solves" these works, as though they were crossword puzzles. Instead I am interested in dealing with questions like, "Why did Henry Adams think these books so special?" "Why did he emphasize their form? his motivations in writing?" "What does give them unity beyond the broad categories of unity and multiplicity?" The techniques which he adopted, and which I wish to dwell on, unify the works and give them meaning page by page; they clarify the literary experiment both as he created it and as he wished it to be read, but without altering the literal meaning of the pages or stretching that meaning to the point of absurdity.

The following chapters, then, seek that direct confrontation with *Mont-Saint-Michel and Chartres* and *The Education of Henry Adams* by concentrating on the works themselves—the motives behind their writing and the unique forms revealed by those intentions. If my primary concern is the thorough investigation of only two works by Adams, it is because they are masterpieces clearly standing apart from the conventional literary forms of his earlier writing and clearly going together as companion pieces. One need not rely upon Adams's word to see that, most simply understood, they contain a thematic unity based on the sharp oppositions between two cultures, two ways of life. And if my approach thus strays from the usual procedure of full-length Adams studies, my forays into other criticism and scholarship will show how much indebted I am to those who have found Adams worth writing about, and who have sustained my own admiration of the artist.

Acknowledgments

For reading all or part of this manuscript, and for giving advice and encouragement in the process, I wish to thank the following: Professors Charles Anderson and Hillis Miller at Johns Hopkins University; Harry Hayden Clark, Merle Curti, and Thomas Tanselle at the University of Wisconsin, Madison; Luther S. Mansfield at Williams College; William Taylor at the State University of New York, Stony Brook; and Robert C. Streeter at the University of Chicago. For financial aid in its writing I want to thank the Samuel S. Fels Foundation and the Graduate School of the University of Wisconsin. For giving personal encouragement I wish particularly to thank my father and mother, John and Mary Simetska Conder; Anna Fusco; Sonya Simetska; and, of course, the person to whom this book is dedicated.

The following publishers ought to be acknowledged for permission to quote from copyrighted materials: Houghton Mifflin Company for permission to quote from *Mont-Saint-Michel and Chartres, The Education of Henry Adams, Letters of Henry Adams, 1858–1891* and *1892–1918* (edited by Worthington Chauncey Ford), and *Henry Adams and His Friends* (compiled by Harold Dean Cater); Constable & Company for permission to quote from *The Education of Henry Adams;* The Macmillan Company for permission to quote from *The Degradation of the Democratic Dogma* by Henry Adams (edited by Brooks Adams, 1919); Alfred A.

Knopf for permission to quote from *The Declaration of Independence* by Carl L. Becker; Harvard University Press for permission to quote from *The Young Henry Adams,* *Henry Adams: The Middle Years,* and *Henry Adams: The Major Phase,* all by Ernest Samuels.

1

The Uniqueness of the *Chartres* and the *Education*

Search for Form

A biographer and historian, a novelist, essayist, and critic of American society and the drift of history at large—all these describe Henry Adams as writer and cosmopolitan intellectual. Although this study is concerned only with those two of Adams's works which rank him as one of America's creative literary geniuses, the spotlight cannot be turned on abruptly without the risk of blinding the reader with its glare. Are his *Chartres* and *Education* indeed to be approached as one would approach a novel, say, or a poem, in order to discover their form—their external and their internal form or, to put it another way, their genre and their methods of handling and organizing the material within? The question, once posed, presents its own apparent difficulties, for they are not novels (he wrote two), nor are they poems (he also wrote two, though they have less literary value), and clearly they differ from the journalistic essays of his youth as well as from the biographies and monumental nine-volume *History* of his mature years.

Perplexing though he may be in thought and style, Adams provided his own clues to unraveling the difficulties of form. He insisted that the books were a unit ("The form of presenting all this . . . was invented in order to make it liter-

ary and not technical"),[1] and to William James he confided
that the *Education* "interests me chiefly as a literary experiment, hitherto, as far as I know, never tried or never successful."[2] If these are literary inventions, the why and the
how of their being can best be understood by contrasting
them to his other works in order to absorb the logic of their
creation before apprehending their individual genius and
beauty.

The wide range of earlier genres in which Adams worked
exposes by contrast the uniqueness of his greatest literary
productions and raises a fundamental question whose answer explains their invention: Why these shifts in genre?
The problem has barely been touched. Interested writers
have highlighted the unity of his thought, despite the different genres in which it was expressed, by emphasizing one or
another of several related themes. This discovery of a coherent world is not unusual, for every writer has his world; but
most bring it into sharpest focus by perfecting their vision
within a single genre, whereas Adams apparently dispersed
his energies among a variety of forms. Many years ago
R. P. Blackmur praised Adams for this very reason—for
maintaining a consistency of vision, "a singular unity of
conception and a striking definiteness of form,"[3] in spite
of the diverse genres he employed. He thought it remark-
able that Adams could sustain a private vision whether he
wrote a biography or a novel, although the demands of
each are considerably different. Admittedly, Blackmur con-
fined himself to explaining Adams's sense of failure (Adams
searched for a unity which could not be contained within

[1] Letter to John Franklin Jameson, 20 March 1909, in *Henry Adams and His Friends: A Collection of Hitherto Unpublished Letters,* ed. Harold Dean Cater (Boston, 1947), p. 650. Hereafter cited as Cater.

[2] Letter to William James, 11 February 1908, in *Letters of Henry Adams: 1892–1918,* ed. Worthington Chauncey Ford (Boston and New York, 1938), 2:490. Hereafter cited as Ford by volume (1 or 2).

[3] "The Expense of Greatness: Three Emphases on Henry Adams," *Virginia Quarterly Review* 12 (July 1936): 404.

the finitude of any one literary form), but his observations point to a new and literary significance for the apparent impatience Adams exhibited in this respect. Given the consistency of his themes, it appears that a good part of his development depended upon trying to find the correct form for their expression; attention to the possibilities a literary form offered him is therefore as important as attention to the ideas he was trying to embody. Not that Adams's world remained static. Obviously there was growth in the thinker; but there was also growth in the artist. For Adams the two were inseparable, so that as his attitude toward fundamental issues changed, so too did the forms of his communication.

What we seek is the logic behind Adams's invention of unique literary structures; and to see him turning from genre to genre in a search for form, we need the ultimate issue underlying all his works. Critics have perceived many[4] and, though none are mutually exclusive, for Adams the best choice is one he himself approved as the formative principle of his thought—precisely because he used so many of the materials of his own life and work in what has ingenuously been called an autobiography. Even if this basic

[4] It is difficult to put in capsule form the central issue behind Adams's work as presented in J. C. Levenson's *Mind and Art of Henry Adams* (Boston, 1957), precisely because Levenson tries to show all the strands of Adams's complex thought affecting a single work, as well as earlier works affecting the later ones. George Hochfield's *Henry Adams: An Introduction and Interpretation* (New York, 1962) finds the essential pattern as the search for an ideal, with the consequent failure of that ideal. D. S. R. Welland has pointed out that Adams needed to turn from the study of character in the novel to the study of force, which required the abandoning of character and the use of a scientific type in the *Education,* thus suggesting a movement from free will to determinism: "Henry Adams as Novelist," *Renaissance and Modern Studies* (University of Nottingham) 3 (1959): 25–50. Ernest Samuels frequently alludes to the issue of free will and determinism: see especially *Henry Adams, The Major Phase* (Cambridge, Massachusetts, 1964), p. 209.

concern had not been consciously with him from the beginning, it would not matter a bit. Adams was introspective enough to become aware of his own larger patterns of thought after they were in operation, and the *Education,* seen simply as a document, bears witness to this. Its central focus, everywhere apparent but nowhere more explicit than in the two prefaces and the concluding theory of history, is a debate over whether man has free will or is determined, an issue at once limited to the individual and symbolically extended to a nation, a world, and the race and its movement of thought. The failures of a manikin imply the failures not only of an age but of human will itself.

The fundamental issue of the *Education* would be the fundamental theme of his whole career, then, even if the book's central interest had not been consciously with him throughout. But, in fact, nearly every important interpreter of Adams's thought has observed how early in his development the issue—a determinism denying free will—confronted him and how persistent was its attraction.[5] Although not yet a determinist at twenty-five, he was so visibly impressed by the possibilities of transforming history into a science that he was prompted to write his brother, "I believe every part of organic nature will be brought some day within this law"[6]—a single law applying equally to man and nature. At forty-six, only half done with his *History* and still not totally committed to a determinist position, he was nonetheless confident "that in another generation psychology, physiology,

[5] See Levenson, p. 26. See also Ernest Samuels, *The Young Henry Adams* (Cambridge, Massachusetts, 1948), pp. 16 ff. Samuels is concerned to show that with his early loss of religion Adams did not immediately adopt a naturalistic position. "He continued to adhere almost desperately to a philosophy of quasi-idealism" (p. 17). Nonetheless, the issue was latent, despite his noncommitment. Obviously Adams was influenced by Comte and Spencer (Samuels, *The Young Henry Adams,* p. 135), and, in the *Education,* chose to slant his point of view to bring the issue into bold relief.

[6] Quoted in Samuels, *The Young Henry Adams,* p. 131.

and history will join in proving man to have as fixed and
necessary development as that of a tree; and almost as unconscious."[7] The artist of the *Education* did not deceive his
readers on the fundamental pattern of his life and thought.
Little wonder that he should have attempted scientific hypotheses of history which critics have alternately admired as
metaphor and belittled as fact. Small wonder, indeed, that
the issue should have remained alive to the very end, for in a
sense it was with him from the very beginning, inherited at
birth. Henry's brother, Brooks Adams, has eloquently testi-
fied to the philosophical pessimism which overtook their
grandfather, John Quincy Adams, in his defeat by Jackson
in 1828.[8] It was more than a personal failure; it shook a
universe ruled by a deity whose laws man could consciously
observe. After 1828, questions arose which showed the old
faith was gone. Is there a deity? Are there laws, and what
kind? Can man consciously work with or against them? At
his birth ten years later Henry Adams had these questions
passed along to him as part of the "eighteenth-century inheritance which he took with his name" (*E*, chap. 1, p. 7).[9]
And little of the arbitrary would enter were the reader to
see some connection between the forms of literary endeavor
he followed and his changing attitudes toward determinism.
It is the basic issue of his career. What remains is to link it
to form.

Henry Adams conducted his first major literary effort as
a political writer covering the Washington scene between
1868 and 1870, those formative years which were to set a

[7] Letter to Francis Parkman, 21 December 1884, Cater, p. 134.
[8] Introduction to *The Degradation of the Democratic Dogma*, ed.
Brooks Adams (includes: "The Tendency of History," "The Rule of
Phase Applied to History," and "A Letter to American Teachers of
History" by Henry Adams) (New York, 1919).
[9] Throughout this study references to *The Education of Henry
Adams* will be made in the text. The edition used is Houghton Mifflin
(Boston and New York, 1918).

pattern of corruption and corporate Caesarism for the nation. He published chiefly in the *Nation* and the *North American Review,* his subjects ranging from the Legal Tender Act to civil service reform, from the scandalous attempts of Jay Gould and James Fisk to corner the gold market to reviews of the record of Congress. Whatever his subject, Adams's aim was reform, and it was particularly on his congressional review, which he called the "Session" in hopes that it would become an annual affair, that he pinned his hopes for becoming a constructive voice in the land. As he later put it in the *Education,* "such a power, once established, was more effective than all the speeches in Congress or reports to the President that could be crammed into the Government presses" (17, pp. 258–59). His failure was as dismal as his ideals were lofty, though it was not without its usual educational value. "The moral law had expired" (18, p. 280). Gone forever was "the eighteenth-century fabric of *a priori,* or moral, principles" (pp. 280–81).

In the absence of positive social results, literary critics now view his journalism as a prelude to art, finding in an essay like "The New York Gold Conspiracy" that same careful attention to character delineation and plot construction for which more than one of his contemporaries acidly gave him credit.[10] The same talent was to serve Adams well when he wrote the sensational, popular novel *Democracy.* Critics also point out how logical it was for the disillusioned reformer to redirect his interests from the present to the past, from the Grant administration to Jefferson's and Madison's, since the fate of Jeffersonian idealism now seemed to parallel his own.[11] But viewed against the backdrop of the

[10] See, for example, Samuels's approach to "The Gold Conspiracy" in *The Young Henry Adams,* pp. 196 ff. On p. 201, Samuels points out the tart contemporary response to Adams's journalism.

[11] See Hochfield, p. 10. On p. 9, Hochfield makes a point about persuasion which I pursue with an emphasis upon literary form and Adams's movement toward determinism.

fundamental issue in Adams's career, this lesson in failure had more telling literary values as well. Intimately connected with his desire for reform was the literary problem of persuasion, the chief goal of any journalistic essay. An attempt to persuade implies that men have the will to make choices for the good, a will which Adams buttressed by enlivening abstract argument with the concrete drama of a morality play. In his essays brilliant caricatures of men like Gould and Fisk were intrinsic to a scenario in which powerful figures consciously chose evils against which his audience should react. The general will to good ought to prevail against the evil of the few.

His own experience taught him otherwise; so it is not surprising that he despaired that the powers of corporate finance made even the very principles of reform irrelevant to American life. "The discussion of so large a subject is matter for a lifetime, and will occupy generations," he wrote. "The American statesman or philosopher who would enter upon this great debate must make his appeal, not to the public opinion of a day or of a nation . . . but to the minds of a few persons who . . . attach their chief interest to the working out of the great problems of human society under all their varied conditions."[12] Society already possessed its own irresistible motion which the best minds of a generation could not reverse—at least not within a generation. Hence abandoning the role of reformer meant abandoning a special literary form, but not his essential idealism, which Adams now approached in a new way, a way allowing impersonal evaluation freed from the demands of formal persuasion.

The new forms, biography and history, were perfectly suited to the goal. Being by their very nature studies of man's will in a larger environment, they had the further advantage of distance—a removal from the chaotic present to a com-

[12] As quoted by Samuels, *The Young Henry Adams*, pp. 200–201.

pleted past which might act as a test tube in which to measure man's control over his destiny. Besides the nine-volume *History of the United States during the Administrations of Thomas Jefferson and James Madison* (1889–91), Adams published three biographies: *The Life of Albert Gallatin* (1879), *John Randolph* (1882), and *The Life of George Cabot Lodge* (1911). For my immediate purposes the *Randolph* and the *Lodge* can be dispensed with. Both belong to Adams's world, but the *Gallatin* displays Adams's method as a historian more clearly than the *Randolph,* a study of perverted idealism; and, by virtue of its subject matter and earlier date, it provides a link with the *History* which the *Lodge* obviously cannot give.[13]

Both the *Gallatin* and the *History* provided ample range for an investigation of idealism, with the pessimistic notes of the one broadened into the full orchestration of the other. *Gallatin* proceeded from a Rousseauistic faith in the American future to total disillusionment, and the *History* studies on a far vaster scale how poorly man can shape his world according to his desires. The failure of Gallatin's fiscal policy undermined the hopeful theories of Jefferson's secretary of the treasury. Jefferson's failure was broader, though not more poignant. The failure of his embargo, the involvement of the nation in war under Madison, destroyed his hopes that America might be exempt from the evils of foreign entanglement.

[13] George Cabot Lodge, the son of Henry Adams's friend, Henry Cabot Lodge, desired to be a poet, but he died early, with only a minor body of work completed. Because its theme is art, the *Lodge* is less suitable than the *Gallatin* for showing a relationship to the *History.* Gallatin was Jefferson's secretary of the treasury and, like Jefferson himself, a spokesman for republicanism and a severe critic of the fiscal policy of the Federalists. As for the *Randolph,* it did not display Adams's method of an exhaustive collection of facts. Levenson has suggested (p. 99) that by the time of its writing, Adams had gained enough recognition so that he did not need to display facts quite so thoroughly as he did with the *Gallatin.*

If the subject matter asked the question, "Can ideals flourish?" it also provided its own negative answer. The internal form of the works is far more interesting because it suggests why ideals cannot be sustained or, to broaden the issue, why man cannot enforce his will upon the world. Affected by the scientific methodology of the German historian Ranke, who wished to recreate the past as it had happened through an exhaustive collection of facts, Adams played the role of passive historian, minimizing interpretation and generalization, letting the documents speak for themselves as much as possible. The *History* supplemented the Rankean ideal with influences from Herbert Spencer and Auguste Comte. A system of analogies and allusions reduced the past to a movement of forces, a Spencerian ideal complemented by viewing the period from 1800 to 1815 as Comte himself might have seen it—as a vital, because formative, historical phase in the national life; a phase whose forces challenged not only the great men of that period but succeeding generations of men as well. With or without these embellishments, however, both books pitted man against external forces, with the forces emerging omnipotent.[14]

In these works Adams moved away from an idealism embodied in a literary form designed to persuade and took up a study of idealism employing a kind of laboratory method—the scientific collection of facts. The new study had two important implications. The first, of course, is that the works, viewed as investigations of free will, lead to determinist conclusions. At first sight, such a conclusion seems to depend upon the subject matter alone. If these idealists failed, were there not others who succeeded? But Adams's method was easily reversible, equally applicable

---

[14] For extensive treatment of the *History*, see William Jordy, *Henry Adams, Scientific Historian* (New Haven, 1952), especially chapters 3–4; Ernest Samuels, *Henry Adams: The Middle Years* (Cambridge, Massachusetts, 1958), especially chapter 10; Levenson, chapter 4.

to success or failure. Like Comte, he would insist that success is not a function of the will of individuals but of their roles as "proper organs of a predetermined movement."[15] The attempted objectivity of Adams's method might also be questioned. Did he not select the facts and provide the embellishments for his work? He could answer fairly that perhaps impartiality is impossible to achieve; but once again, if all the facts were known and presented "correctly," the human will, whether successful or thwarted, was forever accountable to a larger framework of forces determining the appearance of success or failure.

If the first implication of the method is that man is determined, there remains a more vital meaning to be extracted from Adams's writing of biography and history—one which he himself later absorbed to the full. In his able analysis of the *History,* William Jordy observes that "Adams's scientific point of view . . . stemmed from his belief in the historical facts as hard cores of certainty existing outside the mind of the historian."[16] As a measure of Adams's commitment to the Rankean ideal, the comment is significant. It gains immeasureably in importance when the reader recalls that in the pages of the *Education,* when Henry Adams tells of embarking upon his new project, the study of force to be embodied in the *Chartres* and the *Education,* he does so by explicitly juxtaposing the method of these books with the earlier *History* in order to reject the Rankean approach:

He had even published a dozen volumes of American history for no other purpose than to satisfy himself whether, by the severest process of stating, with the least possible comment, such facts as seemed sure, in such order as seemed rigorously consequent, he could fix for a familiar moment a necessary sequence of human movement. [25, p. 382]

[15] Quoted in Samuels, *The Middle Years,* p. 356.
[16] Jordy, p. 13.

That the external forms of the later works are different from the *History* need hardly be mentioned. What must be stressed is that their methods—their relationships to "fact," for example—were deliberately antithetical to the Rankean method of the *History* and were shaped by the determinism to which his mind was nearing commitment.[17]

In the works of his old age Adams did not abandon the didacticism of his youthful essays or that desire to fix a starting point in society from which future progress might be measured which was one goal of the *History*. The motives were enlarged, the starting point moved to an earlier date and a different culture, his search for historical generalizations shifted from the social to the physical sciences, but his aim remained the same: to understand man in relation to the forces surrounding him. The novels played a useful role in his finally realizing this goal as brilliantly as he could. In each, a heroine searches for an ideal which fails her— religion in *Esther* (1884) and the American political process itself for Madeleine Lee in the earlier novel *Democracy* (1880). As prefigurations of the *Chartres* and the *Education* the novels can readily be merged thematically into Adams's world; as forms they have even greater significance. First, the novel as genre liberated him from that fidelity to fact which biography and history demanded and, by so much, moved him toward a world in which "one is trying to catch not a fact but a feeling" (*C*, p. 14),[18] or a world in which, though the "actual journey may have been quite different, . . . the actual journey has no interest for education. The memory was all that mattered" (*E*, 3, p. 43). Fictional techniques affected even the *Chartres* and the *Education*.

[17] See John C. Cairns, "The Successful Quest of Henry Adams," *South Atlantic Quarterly* 57 (Spring 1958): 168–93, for a different though complementary view of the movement of Adams's thought and works.

[18] Throughout this study references to *Mont-Saint-Michel and Chartres* will be made in the text. The edition used is Houghton Mifflin (Boston and New York, 1933).

The internal ordering of the novels is just as instructive in understanding their role in Adams's total development as a writer. In form the books are polemical (a fact which has provoked charges that the characters are mere representations of ideas) and it is on this basis indeed that their importance to Adams's literary growth must be judged. Their numerous discussions of the values of democracy, religion, and science gave Adams that practice in combining narrative and didactic motives intrinsic to his last works. But there the similarity stops, since the *Chartres* and the *Education* operate within a deterministic framework and the novels do not; and the last works are more successful in combining the double motives than *Democracy* and *Esther*.[19]

Both novels involve a quest after ideals. As long as the author still believed in free will he could display this quest, showing his characters making ethical choices, without running into the dilemma upon which naturalistic writers were often impaled. A major interest in the novel lies in a character's ability to choose freely, an interest undercut by the necessity of showing forces determining these characters' choices. In his novels, Adams was on the verge of determinism, for both heroines, by their own free choice, abandon the only ideals available to them, and it remained only to explain why these ideals cannot function. When that explanation came, in the *Chartres* and the *Education,* Adams's center of interest changed. He was no longer interested in character but in the forces which deny men the possibility of choice and reduce them to the level of mere manikins. The novelist's interest in character was thus replaced by the

[19] Fine evaluations of these novels are given in R. P. Blackmur, "The Novels of Henry Adams," *Sewanee Review* 50 (1943): 281–304; Levenson, pp. 85–97 and 199–204; Hochfield, pp. 24–33 and 44–54; and Welland. Welland and Hochfield are particularly good, the former making a valuable point mentioned in footnote 4, above, the latter stressing an analogous point that the thought in these novels leads to explaining the historic process according to an absolute.

scientist's interest in force.[20] The autobiographical pose of the *Education* provided the form and the manikin. As he said in its 1907 preface, "The object of study is the garment, not the figure" (p. x).

This explanation for his abandoning the novel as form is most convincing when one recognizes Adams's own interests and talents. He sent the aspiring writer George Cabot Lodge, who later became the subject of one of the biographies, this telling commentary on the novel:

To me, a story-teller must be a trivial sort of animal who amuses me. His first quality should be superficiality; for this quality, as a fundamental, I take Miss Austen and generally the women-women, not the men-women like George Eliot, as examples . . . . Balzac tires me from the instant he becomes moralist. You know all this. I don't insist. Art comes in . . . when you want to get a moral into me without my knowing it.[21]

Now the moral, or meaning of the work, emerges all too clearly in Adams's novels. Plot and character—these latter "superficialities" which are the very heart of the novel, fail to provide a rich enough texture in *Democracy* and *Esther* to prevent the reader from feeling that Adams is repeatedly hitting him over the head rather hard with the moral: religion, like democracy, was at last only a function of the ego. But with the *Chartres* and the *Education,* the situation is different, for there he achieved a form more congenial to his temperament and talents. In any conventional sense neither work possesses that "dramatic *mise-en-scène*" which, with reference to the *Education,* Adams declared, "I denied to myself."[22] Their "superficialities" consist of the travel book–cultural history guise of the *Chartres* and the autobiographical pose and personal view of world affairs in

[20] On this point see Welland and also Blackmur, "The Novels of Henry Adams," p. 283.
[21] 22 April 1903, Cater, p. 542.
[22] Letter to Barrett Wendell, 12 March 1909, Cater, p. 645.

the *Education.* Their artistry depends upon his making these poses convey a determined movement in history without, as in the novels, belaboring the reader with his meaning. So according to Adams's own terms, the reader is likely to discover more artistry in his last productions than in the more conventional form of the novel.

There remain only two other works of special relevance to Adams's search for form, the *Memoirs of Marau Taaroa, Last Queen of Tahiti* (1893) and the three scientific essays collected and published posthumously by Henry's brother, Brooks, under the title, *The Degradation of the Democratic Dogma* (1919). As a potpourri of art, history, politics, social customs, and the like, *Tahiti* is the experimental format of the *Chartres* and the *Education,* just as its view of change, for the worse, anticipates their historical perspective. There are other similarities. The rise and fall of the House of Teva parallels the decline of the Virgin in the *Chartres* and the Adamses in the *Education.* An emphasis upon the power of women is pronounced in all these works. And Adams's view that "the real code of Tahitian society would have upset the theories of the state of nature as thoroughly as the guillotine did"[23] prophesied those reevaluations of his eighteenth-century heritage which were to occupy so central a place in the *Education.* But although the ensemble had been brought together, the music had yet to be played. The narrator of the *Memoirs* may foreshadow the narrator of the *Chartres* and the *Education,* but her limitations inhibited the sophisticated development of a persona and related strategies created especially to systematize those books' point of view. The tragedy of *Tahiti* still depended upon the ignorance, stupidity, and basic evil of men, not on impersonal force.

As for *The Degradation of the Democratic Dogma,* its least important essay is "The Tendency of History," which Adams prepared in 1894 as an address delivered in absentia

[23] As quoted by Samuels, *The Major Phase,* pp. 105–6.

to the annual meeting of the American Historical Association, of which he had just been elected president. The essay is a kind of window breaker designed to shake the academic mind out of its lethargy and set historians seeking for a scientific view of history—not, it must be added, the scientific methodology of a Ranke, but a scientific view which would bring history under the domain of some generalization as rigorous as those of the physical laws of matter. The main importance of the essay here is its date. It shows that long before the *Chartres* and the *Education* were written, Adams was interested in a new scientific approach which would prove man a determined creature in an impersonally ordered universe.

The other two essays in the volume were composed after his great writings had been completed; but, unlike "A Letter to American Teachers of History" (1910), "The Rule of Phase Applied to History," written and revised between 1908 and 1912, was not printed until after Adams's death. Both are rather experimental in nature, the "Rule" attempting to apply Willard Gibbs's theory of phase in matter to the movement of history, the "Letter" using Lord Kelvin's second law of thermodynamics—the law asserting the degradation of energy within the universe—as a guide for understanding past history and predicting the future. In neither essay does Adams beguile himself with the notion that he is being in the least scientific, in the manner of the physicist or the chemist. Instead, he experimentally uses scientific notions as analogies to explain historical development. His only dogmatism is the assertion that someone must indeed attempt to bring history under scientific law, although he recognized his own inability to do so with anything more than suggestive results.

The goal of all these essays, to derive historical analogies from physical science, reflected a longer standing interest in wedding science and history. It is of even greater interest that Adams specifically associated two of his essays, the

"Tendency" and the "Letter," with his books and clearly thought his rendering of "Rule" was also complementary to them. The publication dates of both books show how they relate to this interest in science. The *Chartres* and the *Education* were privately printed in 1904 and 1907 respectively, for a limited circle of selected readers. (The earlier work was offered to the public in 1913; the *Education,* not till shortly after Adams's death in 1918.) Thus the two major books exist in a scientific context, falling between the early essay, the "Tendency," and the more developed notions of the "Rule" and the "Letter." From the point of view of form, furthermore, they appear in an even more interesting context. On the one hand, the *Tahiti* forecasts the personalized cultural history approach of the late works. On the other, the last essays suggest a scientific approach. It would thus seem very likely that both masterpieces, as literary forms, were animated by a compound of cultural and scientific interests distinguishing them from all his previous writings.

The Intentions of the Artist

Interrelations between literary form and determinism have thus far been emphasized to suggest that Adams's literary career centered upon a search for the proper vehicle to embody his progressively developing view of the world. By the first decade of this century the component ideas of this view had expanded far beyond Washington; indeed, beyond the early years of the American republic into the remotest past and the infinite future. Adams never lost his fervid interest in history; but for him history took on its all-inclusive meaning—that which was, is, and shall be. Science and philosophy might help to give it shape and direction, if it had any, but a literary form was needed to give it plastic and visible expression. The ideas of a lifetime, enshrined in his letters, had to flow together. Little wonder that in the long period of latency before he began the *Chartres* he alluded to the possibility of a book of travels, "a sort of ragbag of everything; scenery, psychology, history, literature, poetry, art."[24] But the man who always "stickled for form,"[25] as his brother Brooks later commented, could hardly rest content with anything so amorphous; and so *Mont-Saint-Michel and Chartres* and *The Education of Henry Adams* finally were born.

Any reader or critic who wishes to learn the multiplicity of motives behind their creation must depend heavily upon the definitive biography by Ernest Samuels, who observes repeatedly how much that was unpremeditated Adams read into his work after the books were completed; but certain facts seem sure. The scale may have been broadened, but when he took up his pen to write the *Chartres* Adams was still keenly interested in the movement of history or, as he would put it, in the relation of man to force. The contradictions between free will and determinism may have tortured his spirit, but as he wrote *Mont-Saint-Michel and Chartres* he was as confirmed a historical determinist as he ever would be. Just as his brother Brooks accepted the dictates of mechanistic determinism in *The Law of Civilization and Decay* (1895), Henry Adams more lyrically refuted the believers in social Darwinism in his sequel to Brooks's study.

The charge is true that Henry Adams was far from accurate in the *Education* when he contended that the two books were conceived together. According to Samuels, "His conception of the relation of the *Chartres* to some work yet to be written apparently arose . . . after he had begun the *Chartres* and not before, and that work had already begun to take shape . . . at least as early as 1899. . . . The moment when his scheme [to write the *Education*] crystallized remains obscure."[26] This fact, however, in no way means that the two books ought not to be read as a unit. If the first line

24 Letter to John Hay, 9 January 1892, Cater, p. 263.
25 Introduction, *Degradation*, p. 7.
26 Samuels, *The Major Phase*, p. 312.

of the *Education* was not in mind when he began the *Chartres*, the *Education* at least was written against the backdrop of the earlier work, and the issue of premeditation is quite irrelevant to an artist exercising poetic license to draw attention to their unitary nature. Indeed, both books seem the unpremeditated crystallization of his ideas during the 1890s, if the letters are evidence, since long before the appearance of the late works the dichotomies of what he came to call unity and multiplicity were already attracting his mind, demanding explanation.[27] But even during the writing of the *Education*, Adams made it clear that he was composing with the *Chartres* in mind. In January 1905, nearly a year before completing the *Education*, he wrote a former student, the medieval historian Henry Osborn Taylor, that he was searching for a formula for anarchism. With his usual stimulating sense of high drama, he declared modern society was less than a century away from total disintegration—perhaps only fifty years at most.

This was the point that leads me back to the twelfth century as the fixed element of the equation. From the relative unity of twelfth-century conceptions of the Prime Motor, I can work down pretty safely to Karl Pearsen's [sic] Grammar of Science or Wallace's Man's Place in Nature, or to Mack [sic] and Ostwald and the other Germans of today. By intercalating Descartes, Newton, Dalton and a few others, I can even make almost a time ratio. This is where my middle-ages will work out.[28]

---

[27] Henry Adams was especially interested in his brother Brooks's *Law of Civilization and Decay* (London, 1895), and conceived of his own late works as more comprehensive sequels to that book (see *Education*, pp. 360–61). Before writing either the *Chartres* or the *Education*, however, he showed great interest in the work, an interest formulated according to familiar dichotomies—"society as a balloon, liable to momentary collapse," which suggests a movement from the unity of an older culture to a multiplicity created by acceleration gone mad. See especially letters in Ford, 2: 70, 76–77, 80–81; and Cater, pp. 495–96.

[28] 17 January 1905, Cater, p. 559.

There is no reason to doubt the validity of his assertion, therefore, that "The two volumes go together, as I think of them, and the one is meaningless without the other."[29]

A more meaningful problem is Adams's repeated claims that the volumes were experiments, in two different ways. First, he called them efforts to write history according to laws derived from physical science. Hence he wrote to Raphael Pumpelly, his geologist friend: "The volume [*Mont-Saint-Michel*] began the demonstration of the law which this *Letter* ["A Letter to American Teachers of History"] announces, and the *Education* illustrates."[30] Less difficult to understand in a man who "stickled for form" was his assertion that the volumes were experiments in literary form. The theme of literary experimentation appears most prominently in his letters concerning the *Education*, as when he announced to William James, "It interests me chiefly as a literary experiment,"[31] but he included *Mont-Saint-Michel* in the same framework when he pointed out: "The form of presenting all this, from the 12th Century till today . . . was invented in order to make it literary and not technical."[32] Such an ambitious combination of scientific and literary motives suggests that Adams meant the volumes to display his later scientific theorizing, but in a literary mode without the necessity of resorting to abstraction.

No one would deny that problems of literary form haunted him. That scientific intentions were intimately connected with these problems is not in itself startling. And that Adams would associate both books with an essay like his "Letter to American Teachers of History," written after the *Education* and paralleling the historical movement with the physical laws of entropy, need cause no consternation. Adams might very well have been acquainted with Lord

[29] Letter to John William Burgess, 13 June 1908, Cater, p. 609.
[30] 19 May 1910, Ford, 2: 542.
[31] 11 February 1908, Ford, 2: 490.
[32] Letter to John Franklin Jameson, 20 March 1909, Cater, p. 650.

Kelvin's second law of thermodynamics before writing the books, or at least during the writing of the *Education,* and its influence would thus appear in his literary treatment of at least one book. Similarly, the physicist Willard Gibbs's Phase Rule, from which Adams drew inspiration when he wrote his own "Rule of Phase Applied to History," apparently would have influenced him—in the *Education* at least. Although the essay was written later, Gibbs is mentioned in chapter 31 of the book. But when Ernest Samuels observes that Adams had only heard about Lord Kelvin in passing, so to speak, while writing the *Chartres;* when he demonstrates that Adams investigated entropy only after completing the *Education;* and when he proves that Adams had confused Willard Gibbs with Wolcott Gibbs, an earlier Harvard associate, and could never have heard of the Phase Rule at the time (the intervention of Adams's editor, who changed "Wolcott" to "Willard," saved Henry some posthumous embarrassment), then Adams's declared scientific intentions naturally become nothing less than suspect. As Samuels points out, neither the *Chartres* nor the *Education,* "contrary to a common misconception, adopted the analogy of thermodynamic entropy."[33] Adams's last essays relating history to the physical sciences may be fascinating, but "because of the common misunderstanding of the successive stages of Adams's thought and the tentative nature of the successive formulations of his theories the later ideas have commonly been read back into the earlier ones."[34] No one encouraged this more than Henry Adams himself.

Why? And what then do we make of his professed motives? First, recall that the last part of Adams's career centered not upon the scientific methodology of Ranke, but on an interest in establishing historical laws as precise as those of science—and even derived from those of science. "The

[33] Samuels, *The Major Phase,* p. 418. Jordy (p. 170) also mentions Adams's confusion about Gibbs.

[34] Ibid., p. 495.

Tendency of History" of 1894 was an open declaration of this new interest. Although it affected his writing, the interest did not compel serious study until his visit to the Paris Exposition of 1899, where the dynamo captured his imagination as completely as the Virgin of Chartres had done four years before. Thereafter he began those dips into scientific theory and invention which became obsessive after the *Chartres* was completed. But scientific investigations left their mark upon this earlier work as well. True, Samuels observes that "Adams's determination to treat the *Chartres* as fixing a datum point for his dynamic theory of history seems to have been something of an afterthought, the result of his reimmersion in science after the first draft of *Chartres* was finished."[35] But Samuels's investigations show that the last chapter on Thomas Aquinas derived considerable power "from the explosive second thoughts inspired by his industrious reading of the commentaries on the new science."[36] "For more than a year he had tinkered with it while counterpointing his ideas in the latest books on science and the philosophy of science so that it was inevitable that he should feel it more and more a parable of contemporary dilemmas of thought."[37] Saint Thomas's Prime Motor was the medieval equivalent of the dynamo.

Even in the *Chartres,* then, Adams had introduced scientific intentions into his narrative, at least in conclusion. Under these circumstances, he later could justly take the liberty of associating at least one of his essays, "The Tendency of History," with his books. He called the *Chartres* the "second in the series," as Samuels observes, implying that the "Tendency" was consciously written as its prelude.[38] The *Chartres* was not specifically in his mind in

[35] Ibid., p. 307.
[36] Ibid., p. 307.
[37] Ibid., p. 299.
[38] Ibid., p. 344. The well-known letter, part of which Samuels quotes, is in Ford, 2: 546–47.

1894, but even if he incorrectly made the series sound pre-meditated, in terms of what he had actually done, his assertion was true. After all, the "Tendency" asked for a science of history, and the *Education* concluded with his dynamic theory of history. Writing the *Education* against the backdrop of the *Chartres* made that theory relevant to both works.

With equal justice Adams could equate the books with scientific analogies in essays he wrote subsequently, even though he had not been aware of their scientific constructs while writing his masterpieces. The fact is that Henry Adams already possessed strong convictions about history and its movement when he began the *Chartres*. He enshrined these in the special forms of both books, and he gave that movement the best scientific expression he could in the dynamic theory of history concluding the *Education*. Thereafter he searched for any scientific theory which, by analogy, would fit the terms of his books. It is hardly accidental that all three versions of his scientific view of history are broadly equivalent. Whether one reads the dynamic theory in the *Education* or the supplementary essays, the "Rule" and the "Letter," the same basic elements appear: the ideas of phases, forces, and movements of thought in history, all guided by a necessity beyond man's will. Although he could never measure the speed, Adams had long been convinced of the direction of the movement—downward. Not progress but decline was the hallmark of his thought. Thus, although Adams was ignorant of thermodynamic entropy until after he completed the *Education,* Samuels nonetheless observes, "The *Chartres* and the *Education* accepted as axiomatic the loss or diminution of emotion, feeling, and instinct."[39] No wonder Adams seized upon entropy as confirmation of his views. No wonder he could think of both the "Letter" and the "Rule" as complementary to his books. "Each formula-

[39] Samuels, *The Major Phase,* p. 418.

tion," for Samuels, "was but another image, figure, or analogy, a marriage of convenience between idea and symbol to be replaced by more apt and expressive analogies"[40] —analogies, one might add, to the books themselves.

The details of each theory might be different, but the outlines were the same, and not so very new to the man who had abandoned Ranke for Karl Pearson and his *Grammar of Science*. Phase, force, the movement of man's thought according to some predetermined pattern—what were these but concepts out of a past when Spencer and Comte were his guides? Updated concepts, indeed, and couched in the language of physical science, but still old wine in the new bottle of science. Only the earlier possibility of progress had been abandoned, though the mind might still jump.

Why then did Adams associate these later essays with the books? The question is better phrased as, Why *could* he do so? If the artist made his later essays sound part of a premeditated pattern, it was a venial sin committed in the service of a good cause—aiding the reader to understand the literary forms of his books. If the *Education's* dynamic theory fitted them, and this was his conscious intent, then any one of them might serve as well. Their patterns were all the same. The man who conceived of all theories as tentative, and who readily acknowledged his as more fragile than most; the man who ultimately committed himself only to the literary aspects of his books—such a man could very well continue to probe other scientific theories which might complement those literary terms he so painstakingly constructed. For these only would he claim certainty; the certainty of personal experience and personal response enshrined in art.

What then do we make of Adams's professed double motives? The problem reduces itself to a purely literary one, to be understood by the literary critic, as Adams himself

[40] Ibid., p. 496.

confirmed when he commented, "The two volumes have not been done in order to teach others, but to educate myself in the possibilities of literary form."[41] There is here a certain amount of typical recalcitrance in stating his full motives, since his goals seemed to defy circumscription. But these could be conveyed only through the literary mode, and so he naturally stressed the primacy of the literary motive whenever he spoke of the books. "Between artists or people trying to be artists, the sole interest is that of form. . . . The arrangement, the construction, the composition, the art of climax are our only serious study."[42]

The amateur scientist searching for a necessary sequence in history was wise not to rely on the abstract theorizing of his dynamic theory, nor on his "Letter" which he sent out broadside to a host of American historians, nor on his "Rule of Phase," never printed in his lifetime. None of these, as he well knew from a scientist who privately evaluated the "Rule," would satisfy the scientific mind, and he was too well acquainted with historians and their craft to believe that he might convince them, by this method, that he had created a necessary sequence. If necessity was to be his theme, the determinist could convince only as the artist persuades, creating fictional forms with their own internal necessity. As an artist, publically disavowing true science or history in his works (though privately hoping that the books might lead in that direction), Adams might claim with certainty that a determined sequence in history exists.

Only after having removed the books from the arena of historical and scientific reality into the reality of art could Adams toy with the infinite, attempting to conceptualize in scientific terms those historical relations which he could render with precision only in the literary forms of *Mont-Saint-Michel and Chartres* and the *Education*. It is this relationship between books and theory which explains the

---

[41] Letter to Edith Morton Eustis, [February, 1908?], Cater, p. 614.
[42] Ibid.

importance Adams attached to literary form. He simply had to be a good artist to establish his historical relations because he knew he could not render them scientifically. To do the latter, as he concluded in his "Letter," "seems, to an impartial bystander, to call for the aid of another Newton."[43]

To see the books in this way is not to lessen Adams's integrity as an artist but to intensify it—to justify the importance he attached to form and to show the need for understanding the books' literary forms as his ultimate scientific expression. In this view, his commitment to art is equivalent to his commitment to history understood as science. By this view the reader can also understand a third motive of the books, their educational value. In his letters Adams repeatedly despaired that this motive would be perceived. "I trust you will not let yourself be beguiled by the form,"[44] he wrote to one friend. "The nearer we can come to romance, the more chance that somebody will read—and understand," he wrote to another, adding, "But not one reader in a thousand ever understands."[45] And when Brooks Adams published his *Theory of Social Revolution,* Henry commented in more strident tones:

Had it been mine, I think I should have made two separate essays of it, not because they are really separate, but because the average damn fool will say that he cannot see what the U. S. Supreme Court has to do with the French Revolution. This is merely one of my hobbies of arrangement, which never concerns the subject-matter. In regard, however, to this subject-matter, I have no more to say than we have often said . . . . I see in history two social attitudes, the one, that of motion, the other that of station.[46]

As if he were commenting on his own masterpieces, Henry Adams insisted upon the need for understanding relation. In his own works he sought to connect the medieval

---

[43] *Degradation,* p. 263.
[44] Letter to John Franklin Jameson, 20 March 1909, Cater, p. 650.
[45] Letter to Whitelaw Reid, 9 September 1908, Cater, p. 622.
[46] Letter of 22 September 1913, Cater, p. 758.

world with the modern. And to what purpose? "Time is very short, but at any rate our middle-ages are long," he wrote Taylor. "What I most want is an intelligent man of science, a thing I shall never find."[47] So here is the educational aim of the books. The world whose beginnings were in the *Chartres* and which was rocked by crisis in the *Education* demands a scientific explanation of history for its own salvation. Only when man knows what forces are beyond his control will he be able to shape his destiny in some measure—in part by identifying with a predetermined movement of unalterable forces, in part by economizing his energies in this way in order to direct them to amenable forces. Adams's educational intention also blends with his artistic intention. Both point to science.

But of all three goals, only the aesthetic one troubled him. And as a consequence the critic of his art has two inseparable tasks: to expose the broader patterns of the books which logically lead to the patterns of his scientific theorizing, and to evaluate the degree of his literary success in using these patterns to create an aesthetic unity in the works, individually and as a unit. The first task requires the analysis of a narrative which Adams called, with reference to the *Education,* an "experiment of trying to find the exact point of equilibrium where the two motives [literary and scientific] would be held in contact."[48] The three important concepts of force, phase, and that declining movement in history which Adams later associated with entropy will be the chief tools of analysis here, although the details of a gravitational field, important to the *Education*'s dynamic theory of history, will play some role in the analysis of that book.

Within this framework of Adams's intentions and the techniques he used to realize them, are there defects? The

[47] Letter of 17 January 1905, Cater, p. 560.
[48] Letter to Barrett Wendell, 12 March 1909, Cater, p. 646.

problem of evaluation is especially difficult. Works so complex, falling outside the standard genres, are hard to judge, for no established standards exist for measuring their greatness or their deficiencies. Adams may have compared his *Education* to Augustine's and Rousseau's *Confessions,* but did either of these exist within a larger unit portraying a determined sequence in history? The criteria for evaluation, then, must depend for the most part upon the author's declared intentions and his own standard of taste. But precisely because the works are intriguing for their unique forms and lofty goals, because the man's taste in art was so demanding and his standards so exacting, the critic need not feel stifled by such limitations.

In some ways Adams was his own best critic. One need not always agree with a man given to habitual self-disparagement, but his own complaints about form, directed to the *Education,* must be taken into account. "Now that I have the stuff before me—in clay—I can see where the form fails, but I cannot see how to correct the failures,"[49] he complained. In another letter he helped localize the problem. Part of it was due to his times, inherently part of the *Education* and (in his mind) essentially undramatic; the better part of it was due to the fact that he had to spell out his intentions at all:

When I read St. Augustine's *Confessions,* or Rousseau's, I feel certain that their faults, as literary artists, are worse than mine. We have all three undertaken to do what cannot be successfully done—mix narrative and didactic purpose and style. The charm of the effort is not in winning the game but in playing it. We all enjoy the failure. St. Augustine's narrative subsides at last into the dry sands of metaphysical theology. Rousseau's narrative fails wholly in didactic result; it subsides into still less artistic egoism. And I found that a narrative style was so incompatible with a didactic or scientific style, that I had to write a long supplemen-

[49] Letter to Edith Morton Eustis, [February, 1908?], Cater, pp. 614–15.

tary chapter [really three] to explain in scientific terms what I could not put into narration without ruining the narrative . . . . My experiment of trying to find the exact point of equilibrium where the two motives would be held in contact was bound to be a failure.[50]

Evidently the book's theoretical ending—the shift from a narrative to a scientific terminology, a change from the literary study of relation to a codification of such relations in abstract terms—disturbed his sense of aesthetic unity. In the light of Adams's Faustian goals, however, this stylistic discrepancy is hardly disturbing; indeed, it was impossible to avoid. As an artist he might create a determined, necessary historical sequence, but one of the conditions of his art was that it create a theory, no matter how tentative, transcending art, capable of being tested in the outside world. For universal applicability, only abstract terms would do. The paradox lies in Adams's goal, not in his literary realization of it. According to his own standards, at least he avoided Rousseau's major fault by employing a manikin figure, although this served larger purposes than his aversion to writing in the first person. And if he admitted to the rather noble defect shared with Augustine, for Adams a falling into the dry sands of science rather than religion, at least he did not share what he considered another inconsistency of Augustine's ending. "The Augustinian adjustment seems to be only the Stoic, with a supernatural or hypothetical supplement nailed to it by violence," he wrote Taylor. "The religionists preached it, and called it Faith."[51] Adams's own theory was hypothetical, but he admitted it was; and because his entire narrative logically leads to science, which demands hypothesis, ultimately it did no violence to the artistic integrity of the *Education.*

Readers might share his dissatisfaction with a related

[50] Letter to Barrett Wendell, 12 March 1909, Cater, pp. 645–46.
[51] Letter to Henry Osborn Taylor, 15 February 1915, Cater, p. 768.

aspect of the *Education*'s form. It is not so much the last three chapters as three or four preceding them that may be defective. In the 1918 preface, which Henry Cabot Lodge signed at Adams's request, Adams wrote:

The scheme became unmanageable as he approached his end. Probably he was, in fact, trying only to work into it his favorite theory of history, which now fills the last three or four chapters of the "Education," and he could not satisfy himself with his workmanship. [p. viii]

"Unmanageable as he approached his end." "Trying only to work into it his favorite theory of history." The comments sound as if he believed "the exact point of equilibrium where the two motives would be held together" failed somewhat earlier. Possibly he meant that the narrative style lapsed into scientific terminology far earlier than the point where it could no longer be avoided, but this is hardly likely. Using the materials of his own life for his narrative, he had to include scientific interests toward the end; but the high level of narrative style is nonetheless sustained. Some of the finest lines and allusions appear within the book's last several chapters. Another possibility is that he felt the narrative no longer conveyed the broad patterns of his necessary historical sequence—patterns which were codified in the last three chapters; but, as later analysis will show, this is simply untrue. Later analysis will also demonstrate the most probable explanation. The man who was so eager for his narrative to convey the relations which must be studied scientifically introduced so many examples—personal and historical—symbolic of the movement of history that, in his eagerness, he failed to exercise that cardinal rule of writing which he preached throughout his life: "My criticisms are always simple; they are limited to one word: —Omit!"[52]

Here only did Adams violate the reader's aesthetic sense.

[52] Letter to Emily Ellsworth Ford, 30 March 1886, Cater, p. 160.

Otherwise that necessary movement of force which Adams
sought vainly in the *History* through an exhaustive collection of fact, and which he could not encompass within the
limitations of the novel, came to fruition on the broadest
scale possible through a mixture of the methods of both.
He employed facts, but only as they attracted an uncle and
a manikin. His plot was history itself, a plot thus deprived of
any usual type of fictional character and concerned instead
with the Virgin and with historical figures treated as neither
more nor less real than she. The determinist came into his
own at last, as artist, and his hybrid literary forms blossomed
to give the movement of history that sense of necessary
sequence distinguishing all great art.

2

Mont-Saint-Michel and Chartres:

The Uses of Subjectivity

The Problem of Form

Mont-Saint-Michel and Chartres has provoked irritated criticism from some readers and aroused the admiration of others ever since its publication in 1913. The book has two basic features. It deals with the materials belonging to the discipline of cultural history, and as a history of the medieval period it has been criticized for factual inaccuracy and historical misrepresentation.[1] But it is also a guide book. Its preface fancifully imagines an uncle and his niece departing from New York for a tour of the cathedrals of France, and this intimate tone of the elderly gentleman explaining to a young girl the artifacts of the past and the spirit in which they were created prevails throughout, giving the book the character of a personal appreciation. As an appreciation of the spirit of an epoch in history, the book has been admired to the point where critics contend that Adams came near to establishing a new literary genre. From this angle of vision all the book's failures as cultural his-

---

[1] For criticisms of this kind see Lynn White, Jr., "Dynamo and Virgin Reconsidered," *American Scholar* 27 (Spring 1958): 183–94; Yvor Winters, *The Anatomy of Nonsense* (Norfolk, Conn., 1943), pp. 23–87. For a defense, see Blackmur, "Harmony of True Liberalism: Henry Adams's *Mont-Saint-Michel and Chartres*," *Sewanee Review* 60 (1952): 1–27.

tory are excusable by a kind of poetic license which is certainly permitted any tourist traveling privately.[2]

All the complaints about the book as history center upon its factual inaccuracy. Of course within the text of the *Chartres* Adams repeatedly emphasized that historical "facts" were not his principal concern (for example, 2, pp. 14, 19); and yet, as if anticipating future criticism when the book was offered to the public, he explained by letter to the medieval historian Henry Osborn Taylor, shortly after Taylor had read the privately printed edition of 1904:

Your work is of a totally different kind. I have no object but a superficial one, as far as history is concerned. To me, accuracy is relative. I care very little whether my details are exact, if only my *ensemble* is in scale. You need to be thorough in your study and accurate in your statements. Your middle-ages exist for their own sake, not for ours. To me, who stand in gaping wonder before this preposterous spectacle of thought, and who can see nothing in all nature so iconoclastic, miraculous and anarchistic as Shakespeare, the middle-ages present a picture that has somehow to be brought into relation with ourselves. To you, there is no difficulty in transferring ourselves into the middle-ages. You require serious and complete study, and careful attention to details. Our two paths run in a manner parallel in reverse directions, but I can run and jump along mine, while you must employ a powerful engine to drag your load.[3]

This letter would seem to suggest the experimental nature of the *Chartres*. Taylor did not perceive that aspect of the book. But seen in their full context, Adams's refer-

[2] See Hochfield, pp. 99, 114, and indeed his whole treatment, pp. 100–114. See also Levenson, pp. 235–88, who sees the book open as a mere tour and then become an imaginative journey and a tragic poem. Elizabeth Stevenson, *Henry Adams: A Biography* (New York, 1956), pp. 311–29, and Robert A. Hume, *Runaway Star: An Appreciation of Henry Adams* (Ithaca, N.Y., 1951), pp. 171–93, share this view, although they are less detailed in their treatment.

[3] 17 January 1905, Cater, pp. 559–60.

ences to relativity, scale, and ensemble might at least suggest that the book, given the artistic materials it deals with, ought to be classed as cultural history. Or so one might think. Taylor later reviewed the book after its official publication in 1913. Although he was not deceived by Adams's characteristic self-depreciation regarding seriousness and completeness of study, his review did not even give the book the status of a cultural history. Instead, it observed that although the *Chartres* contained inaccuracies and distortions these could be excused because its author was interested in rendering a private vision of the medieval zeitgeist based upon personal responses to the period's art.[4]

Taylor's reasons for evaluating the book in this way must have been compelling. As cultural history, judging from the complaints it has engendered, the volume falls apart not so much because of its use of generalization—for generalizations are a basic tool of the historian—as because of the nature of the generalizations themselves. In the *Education* Adams subtitled the *Chartres* "a Study of Thirteenth-Century Unity" (1918 preface, p. vii); and of course a major charge against him is relevant at this point, since critics and historians alike call his unity an illusion.[5] Of course in the *Chartres* Adams repeatedly shows his awareness of the con-

[4] *American Historical Review* 19 (April 1914): 592–94. Taylor wrote that we "foregather all the while with Mr. Adams, to our great delight, if not instruction." He added that it was a question "whether Mr. Adams is merged in the Middle Ages, or *vice versa*." The review is sympathetic, but only because the book is seen as Henry Adams's private reactions to the period.

[5] On this point see critics mentioned in n. 1, as well as Oscar Cargill's defense, "The Medievalism of Henry Adams," in *Essays and Studies in Honor of Carleton Brown* (New York, 1940), pp. 296–324. Of critics in n. 1, White and Winters especially criticize Adams's unity as illusory. Carl L. Becker implies such criticism when he says Adams belongs to the metaphysicians rather than to historians, who trace observable phenomena, not underlying agencies. See his Review of the *Degradation, American Historical Review* 25 (1920): 480–82.

tradictions and diversity of the age, finally making the prescient observation:

A Church which embraced, with equal sympathy, and within a hundred years, the Virgin, Saint Bernard, William of Champeaux and the School of Saint-Victor, Peter the Venerable, Saint Francis of Assisi, Saint Dominic, Saint Thomas Aquinas, and Saint Bonaventure, was more liberal than any modern State can afford to be. Radical contradictions the State may perhaps tolerate, though hardly, but never embrace or profess. Such elasticity long ago vanished from human thought. [16, p. 356]

But despite Adams's recognition that his unity was composed of diversity stretched to the point of sheer contradiction, he remains vulnerable on the issue precisely because he found in the Virgin a higher synthesis resolving all contradiction. Educated readers balk at his Mariolatry,[6] at statements like these: "The Virgin was present with a reality that never belonged to her Son or to the Trinity" (10, p. 182). "In the midst of violent disputes on other points of doctrine, the disputants united in devotion to Mary; and it was the single redeeming quality about them" (13, p. 253). "You had better stop here, once for all, unless you are willing to feel that Chartres was made what it is, not by the artist, but by the Virgin" (8, p. 128). With flourishes like this, Adams apparently dismissed church doctrine, the history of philosophy, and architectural criticism. To dismiss objections made to statements of this kind by pointing to

[6] See Reverend H. F. Blunt, "The Maleducation of Henry Adams," *Catholic World* 145 (April 1937): 46–52; Frances Quinlivan, "Irregularities of the Mental Mirror," *Catholic World* 163 (April 1946): 58–65. A dissertation at the University of Wisconsin by Sister Mary Aquinas Healy takes as one main subject Adams's treatment of the Virgin in contrast to the official view of Catholic dogma ("A Study of Non-Rational Elements in the Works of Henry Adams as Centralized in His Attitude toward Women," *Dissertation Abstracts* 16 [1956]: 2163). Nathalia Wright does not balk in "Henry Adams's Theory of History: A Puritan Defense," *New England Quarterly* 58 (1945): 204–10.

the poetic license granted the artist is to run squarely into the problem of Adams's high seriousness.[7] To account for that seriousness, one must show how Adams tried to demonstrate the validity of his generalizations. If their validity cannot be upheld from the points of view of the historian and the scientist, at least they can be seen as valid within the limited context of what Adams called his "scientific" method. The method also is indefensible from the point of view of either historian or scientist; but it does shape the book, and to reveal the unique form of the book is the object of this study.

The Literary Use of Subjectivity

Even a cursory reading of the *Chartres* reveals a striking emphasis upon personal feeling—sometimes a subtle appeal to the emotions of the reader, but just as frequently a flat assertion of the individual responses of the narrator. Although this can be pardoned when one realizes that it is an appreciation of the Middle Ages, the uncle's own insistence that his purpose is light, almost trivial (4, p. 60), and that on a summer tour one can admissibly allow feeling to prevail over fact (5, p. 78) should immediately arouse suspicion that some more serious purpose is concealed by this stance. Any reader of the *Education* recognizes this manner as Adams's favorite literary device, and a reader of his letters knows that Adams enshrined in art what was basic to his personality.

This subjectivity is too pervasive to require extensive citation, but one might observe that it is present in all the crucial turning points of the tour. It begins with the uncle proffering advice, "The man who wanders into the twelfth century is lost, unless he can grow prematurely young," and he immediately identifies youth with sensory acuteness and emotional flexibility (1, p. 2). When he speaks to his

[7] See chapter 1 of this study.

niece of the "Chanson de Roland," he insists that he is "trying to catch not a fact but a feeling" (2, p. 14). And at the
conclusion of the first part of their tour, the uncle prepares
to go to Chartres with a renewed affirmation that might
well define the book's point of view—the compelling need
for feeling to prevail over intellect:

> We have set out to go from Mont-Saint-Michel to Chartres in
> three centuries, the eleventh, twelfth, and thirteenth, trying to get,
> on the way, not technical knowledge; not accurate informa-
> tion; . . . not anything that can possibly be useful or instructive; but
> only a sense of what those centuries had to say, and a sympathy
> with their ways of saying it. [4, p. 60]

Thereafter the tour is marked by a growing sense of immediacy and a more deliberate appeal to emotion. "Now
let us enter," "Now let us look about," the guide beckons
with a kind of hushed expectancy, and once inside Chartres
Cathedral he insists with developing urgency and intensity
that the Virgin's presence can be felt, and that she literally
built the cathedral. Indeed the chapters on Chartres (5–10)
move from a view of the Virgin as symbol to an assertion
of her reality and autonomy, an assertion whose authen-
ticity depends on feeling far more than on intellect. The
transition is not only revealed by statement but is supported
by the situation. For uncle and niece, who began as tourists,
end as pilgrims ("when we rise from our knees now, we
have finished our pilgrimage" [10, p. 195]), and the concluding chapters assume that the reader has also accepted
the reality of the Virgin as an autonomous force, just as
medieval society had done.

To repeat, this kind of emotional response is not really
inappropriate within the context of a summer tour, given
a developed sensitivity to art. What is odd is that Adams
based so many serious judgments upon subjective grounds.
He reversed Viollet-le-Duc's strictures against the architectural merits of the apse at Chartres (7, pp. 124–25); he re-

jected orthodox church interpretations of iconography (5, pp. 7–8); he dismissed with a certain contempt those scholars who maintain that the "Chanson de Roland" could have no reference to the Battle of Hastings in spite of the fact that Wace believed it did when he wrote his "Roman de Rou." ("Poetry was not usually written to prove facts," Adams declared. "Wace wrote a hundred years after the battle of Hastings. One is not morally required to be pedantic to the point of knowing more than Wace knew" [2, pp. 19–20].) And the larger generalizations whose validity Adams proposed are based upon smaller subjective judgments, of which these are only three examples.

Clearly the travel book structure alone cannot explain why Adams—who was a good medievalist himself (recall his teaching days at Harvard), and who spent additional years doing the research for this favorite book of his—should allow appreciation to interfere with scholarly responsibility. And indeed the *Chartres* reveals another side—a wealth of fact and information, a breadth of knowledge which might be staggering were its author not so fine a writer as to wear his learning lightly and gracefully. Upon further investigation one discovers that he uses this knowledge as a kind of "objective" base to support the judgments of imagination. Throughout the volume subjective and "objective" elements subtly merge into a prime artistic strategy which is an important aspect of the book's structure and by which Adams seeks to validate the uncle's generalizations.

Adams lays the groundwork for his strategy in the first chapter by attention to the role of his narrator. There the uncle of the preface, who had just arrived at Madame Poulard's hotel within the grounds of the Mount, subtly merges into what Adams calls "our two hundred and fifty million arithmetical ancestors of the eleventh century" (1, p. 3). Beginning with the light touch of this patent absurdity (England and northern France could have had no more than five million inhabitants), the author soon changes the "one" referring to the uncle alone and the "our" and "we" referring to uncle and niece (or reader [1, pp. 2–3]) to the "we" of identification with eleventh-century Normans: "We never fail to make our annual pilgrimage to the Mount on the Archangel's Day" (1, p. 5). As he departs, furthermore, the uncle plainly implies through Wordsworthian allusion that he is returning to the scenes of his personal childhood eight centuries ago (1, p. 2). The age of the narrator revisiting the culture of his "youth" elevates him into a kind of Gerontion figure representing the experience of the race in its complete historical dimensions.[8]

Although he is the same individual, the man of seventy always recognizes some irreparable break between his hypothetical youth and his actual age; and the narrator of the *Chartres* carries with him a like diffracted consciousness, although here it assumes historic and cultural proportions. Nostalgically he reconstructs the feelings of youth, the spirit of medievalism as he "remembers" it, and at times he almost recaptures it. But not quite. The identification is always tenuous, and reality intrudes to recall a rupture in

[8] In his Wisconsin dissertation ("Symbol and Idea in the Major Works of Henry Adams," *Dissertation Abstracts* 21 [1960]: 623–24) Melvin Ernest Lyon calls his chapter (5) on the *Chartres* "Naturalism and the Childhood of Man" and his chapter (6) on the *Education* "Naturalism and the Fall." His revised work is now at press for publication, so I refer to chapters, not pages, of his dissertation. He observes that the framework of the *Chartres* allows Henry Adams to return to his childhood, where an intuitive method of knowing, as opposed to the inductive method of Adams's scientific theorizing, prevails. Thus the framework of the *Chartres* is the world of reality as opposed to the illusion of the medieval world. Within the *Chartres* there are five points of view, of which the two most important are medieval man's and the narrator's, and the latter shatters illusion. My treatment uses both the framework and a double point of view as a device for analysis to establish a consistent movement, determining structure, dependent upon the narrator's associative method as it relates to the "scientific" experiment. Levenson also treats the tour structure as a device to transform the spatial tour into a drama of time (p. 239).

historical sequence which places this past beyond his reach. Although it underlies much of the feeling of the narrative throughout, particularly in references to lost senses and lost artistic abilities, the rupture is made explicit in several places. Early in chapter 1 Adams insists, "The man who wanders into the twelfth century is lost, unless he can grow prematurely young" (1, p. 2). The tour begins with hope that the past can be recovered; it concludes with a desolate sense of alienation in a moving passage describing the Virgin "looking down from a deserted heaven, into an empty church, on a dead faith" (10, p. 195). What the narrator feels many others had felt, and he thereafter recites from Villon lines of disenchantment, ending his chapter with prose as intense as Villon's poetry: "For the first time since Constantine proclaimed the reign of Christ, a thousand years, or so, before Philip the Fair dethroned Him, the deepest expression of social feeling ended with the word: Despair" (12, p. 248). The same poignant knowledge of loss emerges at the close of the book. Here "was an art marked by singular unity, which endured and served its purpose until man changed his attitude toward the universe" (16, pp. 376–77).

This sense of profound rupture within the book is, of course, one of the important elements always referred to when the book is conceived of as a tragic poem; and certainly Adams's sense of language makes it profoundly moving. But more important is the role of the narrator in this respect. He seeks to bridge the gap, using "objective" methods (his personal knowledge of medieval art) as a foundation for recreating the subjective nature of medieval life. In the process he becomes for the medieval period the collective Western consciousness; and by the method of the book which elevates him to this status, Adams seeks to authenticate the generalizations he makes in this role.

To observe this strategy in operation, "La Chanson de Roland" (chapter 2) can serve as a starting point. Although his subject is the "Roland," Adams devotes more than seven pages to a kind of preamble whose sole purpose is to unite in some inextricable fashion the "Roland" with Mont-Saint-Michel. He establishes a relationship based upon popular tradition incarnated in the work of three poets and in a tapestry:

Through William of Saint-Pair and Wace and Benoist, and the most charming literary monument of all, the Bayeux tapestry of Queen Matilda, we can build up the story of such a pilgrimage which shall be as historically exact as the battle of Hastings, and as artistically true as the Abbey Church. [2, p. 17]

The relationship between the "Roland" and Michael's church is grounded upon a series of associations which exist in medieval art. The tapestry of Queen Matilda depicted Harold the Saxon and William the Norman on the sands before Mont-Saint-Michel. If they were so near they no doubt dined in the refectory where Taillefer, William's jongleur, no doubt sang the "Roland." Critics may dispute whether he could have sung anything but an earlier version, but Adams relies upon the beliefs of poets, who associated the "Roland" so closely with the Mount that a line referring to it was anonymously inserted in the poem. Having established a relationship based on poetry and popular belief, the "objective" part of the chapter, the narrator proceeds to dramatize the singing of this chanson within the refectory. The opening lines, alluding to Charlemagne's Spanish conquest, would have stirred William, who already must have been thinking of the possibility of invading England. Roland's death, an act of homage to God, reflected perfectly the feudal hierarchy of loyalties, and the emotions of an audience would have been conditioned by that fact. The narrator, in short, adopts an associative method to dramatize his story and give significance to the poetry and the architecture; for the one is a mirror of the other. This associative method is a subjective element. But if associative, it is not whimsically free association, because it is held within the matrix of tradition, belief, and poetry itself—the "objective" element of the strategy.

The chapter thus highlights one aspect of Adams's use of "objective" fact with subjective judgment. The historian of course may rightly argue that the "objective" element is hardly that, based as it is upon folklore and popular tradition, rarely the repository of hard, authentic fact. But it is popular belief and feeling which *are* the facts attracting Adams. Later, when discussing popular views of Blanche of Castile and Thibaut-le-Grand, he clarifies his approach:

> For us the poetry is history, and the facts are false. French art starts not from facts, but from certain assumptions as conventional as a legendary window, and the commonest convention is the Woman. The fact, then as now, was Power, or its equivalent in exchange, but Frenchmen, while struggling for the Power, expressed it in terms of Art . . . . To them Thibaut and Blanche were bound to act Tristan and Isolde. Whatever they were when off the stage, they were lovers on it. [11, p. 224]

What the people believed to be true becomes the "objective" matrix within which Adams imaginatively operates, therefore, because belief, whether factually grounded or not, is itself a force affecting behavior and patterns of thought.

Having established such a mold, the narrator proceeds to make further associations within its bounds, recreating the natural associations of the medieval mind in specific situations. This he does at the dinner in the refectory, and it leads him to some unorthodox theological conclusions: "Correct as the law may have been, the religion even at that time must have seemed to the monks to need professional advice," he observes (2, p. 29), for the "Roland" subordinated Christian virtues to military virtues. But even the monks were caught up by the military ardor in a spirit partially contravening Christian principle, he imagines, and he assigns to them the same view of the Mount at which he has arrived. When they heard the invocation of the Mount in the line added to the "Roland," the uncle announces:

One needs no original documents or contemporary authorities to prove that, when Taillefer came to this invocation, not only Duke William and his barons, but still more Abbot Ranulf and his monks, broke into a frenzy of sympathy which expressed the masculine and military passions of the Archangel better than it accorded with the rules of Saint Benedict. [2, p. 31]

This approach does not deny other meanings for the Mount, associations more specifically religious; but it does insist that among several channels of meaning, these associations were also likely, even inevitable; and so when the uncle concludes his tour of Mont-Saint-Michel and arrives at his final generalization about the eleventh century, it too possesses the validity of personal reaction controlled by artistic associations medieval man himself made:

One looks back on it all as a picture; a symbol of unity; an assertion of God and Man in a bolder, stronger, closer union than ever was expressed by other art; and when the idea is absorbed, accepted, and perhaps partially understood, one may move on. [3, p. 45]

This same method of merging "objective" with subjective elements not only expands the role of the narrator but significantly alters the character of those very generalizations for which the book has been criticized. Title as well as content points to a highly detailed attention to art, to which all other events are intrinsically related. Architecture is taken as primary and integrates all possible manifestations of medieval culture. So in chapter 2 the "Roland" is figured as sung within the refectory of the Mount by Duke William's jongleur—the same Duke William who united Normandy with England in 1066. The political unity of the age is complemented by the artistic unity of the Mount and the poetic unity of the "Roland." Unity exists on all planes, proceeding from art and expanding into society, and because they all converge in the mind of the sentient narrator as he responds to art, his expression of these observations within the form of the *Chartres* unites them into an aesthetic whole.

This technique is employed throughout the book, ending in the treatment of Thomism viewed according to architectural analogies established in the early pages, and it is precisely this preoccupation with art which considerably modifies the character of Adams's generalizations and gives to them a special kind of validity. Because the unity of medieval culture he asserts depends for its existence upon the unity of art structures, the *Chartres* is not a critique in the ordinary mode of cultural history; it is an art critique instead, and its unities are aesthetic rather than historical entities.[9]

In order to understand fully how Adams uses subjective and "objective" elements to arrive at aesthetic generalizations, it is wise to recall the nature of the art confronted here. Gothic architecture (and, to a lesser degree, Romanesque) is known for complexity of design; and for both Mont-Saint-Michel and Chartres Cathedral, the possibility of viewing the structures as organic, architectural wholes is complicated by the facts of their construction. Each spans three centuries: Mont-Saint-Michel is a sprawling structure with additions made through the ages as the pressure for larger facilities demanded; Chartres was twice destroyed by fire and rebuilt. Their architects were separated by long spans of time, a century or more, and faced the problem of contributing something unique and consistent with changes in taste yet in harmony with the earlier parts of the structures. Adams's problem was to define logically the

[9] Hochfield's study mentions Adams's intention to use art as a measure of all medieval forces (p. 108), but finds that his "scientific" intention was irrelevant to his use of the materials of art. He treats the emphasis upon art in the book in terms of its basic thematic relationships to Adams's work.

complicated structures whose unity he felt, and he searches for some central control by which to establish the aesthetic and organic wholeness of buildings apparently lacking unity.

The opening chapter of the section on Chartres (5, "Towers and Portals") consists of an argument based upon sound authority and cold architectural fact ineluctably leading to that control. Adams analytically defines the stages in the cathedral's construction, beginning with the old tower, completed by 1150, then notes the fate of this tower, whose proportions were damaged by the introduction of the great rose after the fire of 1194, and shows how the sixteenth-century architect accommodated his new tower to the rose itself. He thus leads the reader to his own conclusion, stated most bluntly in the following chapter. The Virgin was the symbol controlling the church's construction, and the facts of its construction "prove" it. Similarly the doors of Chartres display her prominence first as Byzantine empress, later as French queen.

This argument, the "objective" section, prepares for "The Virgin of Chartres" (6), where the controlling symbol, which had been reached through analytic methods, is developed and presented to the reader through the subjective process. Step by step Adams defines the tastes of Mary as evidenced by a personality revealed in the architecture itself; and through attention to space, light, convenience, and color—the special interests of the Virgin—he establishes the terms by which the aesthetic unity of the cathedral can be judged. Always it must be judged not so much with reference to its own independent organic relationships as with reference to Mary. Hence in "Roses and Apses" (7), Adams can explain the rose window in her own terms: "Conspicuous, then, in the west front are two feelings: respect for the twelfth-century work, and passion for the rose fenestration; both subordinated to the demand for light" (7, p. 115). So, too, he feels qualified to quarrel with Viollet-le-Duc, who called the irregularity of the apse a defect. What the French authority failed to understand were the full dimensions of Mary as symbol. She demanded light even at the sacrifice of form, consistent with her character as an intercessor who would, if necessary, violate the laws of God to secure benefits for man. The next two chapters, "The Twelfth-Century Glass" (8) and "The Legendary Windows" (9), display her influence in the same way, for her personality allowed subjects for windows which traditionally could not be placed in churches, and her private symbols unite what might otherwise be a chaos of glasswork.

With this intuitive understanding of the aesthetic control of the cathedral, Adams leaps from aesthetic to seemingly historical generalizations in "The Court of the Queen of Heaven" (10), the conclusion of the tour as it focuses specifically on the cathedrals. He concentrates upon the rose windows of Blanche of Castile and Pierre de Dreux. "Every one knows that there is war between the two!" (10, p. 183). Yet the political conflict is resolved within the art, an important point for understanding the relationship between art and history in the book. Precisely because the warring factions of society could be harmonized within the terms of art, Adams can contend that the society itself possessed historical unity; its major elements were capable of being synthesized, whereas in the contemporary world, only minor fractions of culture can be encompassed and resolved aesthetically.[10]

This strategy of merging "objective" and subjective ele-

[10] Levenson sees art as unity opposing chaos (p. 325) and Hochfield (pp. 107–9) views Adams's admiration for the art in terms of selfless service to an ideal. For the purposes of the "scientific" experiment, I stress the mode of perception (art is unified, as well as society, through the mind of the narrator) and the transformation of historical into aesthetic generalizations to show how Adams's experiment provided a method for writing the book and created a major strategy affecting structure.

ments, in summary, produces two important effects. First, it elevates the uncle to the role of the collective Western consciousness. Within chapters 1–3, an "objective" matrix consisting of associations made by medieval man within his art is used by the narrator to make associations of his own which are apparently historical in nature. But these same generalizations, because of their focus upon art, assume an aesthetic rather than a historical validity. This transformation can be seen in the chapters on Chartres Cathedral (5–10), where Adams first establishes a symbol and then subjectively displays its aesthetic unifying powers. Still, if this strategy provides a literary movement in the book to alter the apparent significance of both the uncle and his observations, what values of a more universal nature emerge from these pages? Others might make associations different from this uncle, and their aesthetic judgments might considerably diverge from his. The greatest significance of these pages depends upon the "scientific" aims of their author, and they must now be investigated to show the fullest meaning of his strategy.

The Scientific Use of Subjectivity

R. P. Blackmur, in an article on Adams's symbols of Virgin and dynamo, once debated whether Adams also accepted these as objective energies.[11] The *Education* is somewhat equivocal, dismissing the issue with the flat statement: "Symbol or energy, the Virgin had acted as the greatest force the Western world ever felt, and had drawn man's activities to herself more strongly than any other power, natural or supernatural, had ever done" (25, pp. 388–89). But the last essays by Adams confirm Blackmur's conclusion that Adams thought of his symbols as forces too. In fact, he thought them measurable.

Measurement was at the very heart of the problem in his

[11] "The Virgin and the Dynamo," *Magazine of Art* 45 (April 1952): 147–53.

attempt to reduce history to science, for clearly the force of the Virgin did not reduce itself to watts and volts like electricity. Here subjectivity could serve a purpose, for, as the *Education* asserts, "by action on man all known force may be measured" (25, p. 388). Hence in the *Chartres* the power of the Virgin can be presented only through the sentient narrator, an intention Adams made clear in a letter about the book:

I wanted to show the intensity of the vital energy of a given time, and of course that intensity had to be stated in its two highest terms—religion and art. As our society stands, this way of presenting a subject can be felt only by a small number of persons. My idea is that the world outside—the so-called modern world— can only pervert and degrade the conceptions of the primitive instinct of art and feeling, and that our only chance is to accept the limited number of survivors—the one-in-a-thousand of born artists and poets—and to intensify the energy of feeling within that radiant centre. In other words, I am a creature of our poor old Calvinistic, St. Augustinian fathers, and am not afraid to carry out my logic to the rigorous end of regarding our present society, its ideals and purposes, as dregs and fragments of some primitive, essential instinct now nearly lost.[12]

A notion of decline which Adams later associated with entropy underlies the commentary and thus explains many of Adams's procedures throughout the *Chartres*. Seeking to recover the force of the Virgin, lost to the hardened sensibility of modern man, he surrounds himself with as much of her art as is necessary to release the wellsprings of subjective response. Although representing the Virgin's force as it acts upon one man seems hardly scientific, Adams thought subjectivity a tentative means for conducting his experiment.

Reference to the *Education* reveals this "scientific" use of subjectivity. In the scene at the Paris Exposition in "The Dynamo and the Virgin" (25, p. 383), Adams first apprehended the powerful impact of the dynamo operating in

---

[12] To Albert Stanburrough Cook, 6 August 1910, Ford, 2: 546–47.

some way as a force on his mind, a way analogous to the
effect the Virgin of Chartres produced. Blackmur contended
that both dynamo and Virgin operated as force because they
affected, rather than followed, the mode of men's thought.[13]
Certainly they had this kind of impact upon Adams, and
in determining to measure these forces, he recognized that
no absolute standard of value could be erected, precisely
because the impact he sought to define was their fullest cultural effect. With no absolute standard possible, he thought
measurements might be achieved by comparing the effect of
each force on its respective culture. But even this relativity
required a constant, and here the persona of Adams came
into its own for experimental purposes. The *Education*
states it this way:

> The historian was thus reduced to his last resources. Clearly
> if he was bound to reduce all these forces to a common value, this
> common value could have no measure but that of their attraction
> on his own mind. He must treat them as they had been felt; as
> convertible, reversible, interchangeable attractions on thought. He
> made up his mind to venture it; he would risk translating rays
> into faith. Such a reversible process would vastly amuse a chemist,
> but the chemist could not deny that he, or some of his fellow
> physicists, could feel the force of both. When Adams was a boy
> in Boston, the best chemist in the place had probably never heard
> of Venus except by way of scandal, or of the Virgin except as
> idolatry; neither had he heard of dynamos or automobiles or ra-
> dium; yet his mind was ready to feel the force of all, though the
> rays were unborn and the women were dead. [25, p. 383]

The constant in the equation between rays and faith, the
unit of measurement, is the mind of Adams himself; and
when the reader realizes that the narrator of the *Chartres*
is identical with the narrator of the *Education,* he recognizes the manner in which Adams thought the books a "scientific" experiment. Each records in literary fashion the
responses of the same individual to force, and by the power

[13] "The Virgin and the Dynamo," p. 148.

which force exercises in each book upon the same narrator, Adams hoped to establish a relative measurement of the respective strength of the Virgin and dynamo.

That the two personae are identical one can assume from the *Education,* which announces his intention to undertake such an experiment (25, p. 383). Very early in the narrative of the *Chartres,* moreover, an identity between the two is established. The narrator perceives a resemblance between the coasts of Normandy and New England, and he tells his niece: "The relation between the granite of one coast and that of the other may be fanciful, but the relation between the people who live on each is as hard and practical a fact as the granite itself." It is certain "that, if you have any English blood at all, you have also Norman" (1, pp. 2, 3). The visit to Normandy is conceived of as a spiritual return, and with good reason, for the boy of the *Education*'s early pages possesses both English blood and the French of his grandmother, Louisa.

Although Adams's subjectivity hardly constitutes a basis for a true scientific experiment, the patterns of his response, in the light of his "scientific" intentions, give the book a genuine unity of form because they are organized according to the patterns of his later historical theories. Those patterns will be the concern of the rest of this chapter on the *Chartres.*

The Law of Entropy and the Framework of the *Chartres*

By 1902 (he wrote *Mont-Saint-Michel and Chartres* that summer)[14] Adams had long been a veteran marching under the banner of Comte, Buckle, and Spencer—at least in the

[14] My first chapter acknowledges that the law of entropy and the rule of phase were the basis for scientific theories of history created after the writing of *Mont-Saint-Michel and Chartres* and Adams's *Education,* but since Adams saw these as analogues to his works, they provide useful tools for literary analysis. Those theories bring into bold relief literary strategies within a single work and the complementary nature of both works, based upon such strategies.

sense that, if he did not adopt their conclusions, he sought to use their methods. The same might be said of the influence Darwin and Lyell exerted. He rejected Spencer's wholesale application of their thought to social analysis, but he obviously approved using some kind of evolutionary-scientific approach. Quite the opposite of Spencer's, it was evolution in reverse.[15]

Adams derived his theory of social entropy from Lord Kelvin's second law of thermodynamics, the principle of the progressive deterioration of energy, and he gave it form by creating analogies to Willard Gibbs's Rule of Phase. But if these principles applied by scientists exclusively to physical energy were indeed applicable to history, he obviously needed a test tube, a starting point in time from which to measure the decline of social energies through the present day. His treatment of the Middle Ages already had served that purpose. He wrote to A. S. Cook that the *Chartres* was so intended, and that he chose this period "since I could not get enough material to illustrate primitive society, or the society of the seventh century B.C., as I would have liked."[16]

The period had other virtues as well. Adams wanted an inevitable sequence in history, for only that could be scientific. "He had even published a dozen volumes of American history," according to the *Education*, "for no other purpose than to satisfy himself whether, by the severest process of stating, with the least possible comment, such facts as seemed sure, in such order as seemed rigorously consequent, he could fix for a familiar moment a necessary sequence of

[15] For a good basic background of Adams in relationship to the social sciences taking form during his life see Henry S. Kariel, "The Limits of Social Science: Henry Adams's Quest for Order," *American Political Science Review* 50 (1956): 1074–92; and Timothy Paul Donovan, *Henry Adams and Brooks Adams: The Education of Two American Historians* (Norman, Oklahoma, 1961), pp. 35–65.

[16] 6 August 1910, Ford, 2: 546.

human movement" (25, p. 382). Part of his problem in this renewed search for continuity was to discover the logical antecedents of the science dominating his day. Knowing that science had largely abandoned a search for the unity of all energy, or rather approached the problem backward by forever searching for larger and more comprehensive theories to explain phenomena, he sought an era when the unity of all energy was assumed. Religion always assumes this, positing unity in God; and in the Christian era, religion reached its apex in the late Middle Ages. According to Adams, at least, Thomism was the logical beginning of modern science, for what was the Thomistic God but the sum of all energy, and what was medieval religion but a primitive scientific way of controlling it? In his view the theologian was the logical and necessary ancestor of the scientist, and hence Western religion at its highest was the perfect point of departure for a study of Western science rising to its zenith. He told Henry Osborn Taylor as much:

I am trying to work out the formula of anarchism; the law of expansion from unity, simplicity, morality, to multiplicity, contradiction, police. I have done it scientifically, by formulating the ratio of development in energy, as in explosives, or chemical energies. I can see it in the development of steampower, and in the various economies of conveyance. Radium thus far is the term for these mechanical ratios. The ratio for thought is not so easy to fix. I can get a time-ratio only in philosophy. The assumption of unity which was the mark of human thought in the middle-ages has yielded very slowly to the proofs of complexity . . . . This was the point that leads me back to the twelfth century as the fixed element of the equation.[17]

With this kind of equation between religion and science in mind it should be easier to understand the meaning and even the logic behind Adams's statement in the *Education* that "he would risk translating rays into faith," for it

[17] 17 January 1905, Cater, pp. 558–59.

was the inevitable consequence of venturing to bring human history within the scope of physical law. The influence of Comte also showed itself here, for as a unit the *Chartres* and *Education* appear to duplicate Comtean divisions of society (the *Chartres* would obviously represent Comte's religious stage). But the method of these later years is considerably different from the method of the *History*, which also displayed Comtean methods[18] but which represented an entirely different approach stressing objective fact rather than subjective feeling. Because of this new emphasis, Adams's interest in scientific laws of history produced results far more literary than the exhaustive accumulation of facts in the nine-volume study. And the framework of the *Chartres* is intimately connected with this new approach.

The single most important scientific idea later attracting Adams's thought was the law of entropy, an idea which seemed supported by his own observations on economy in the *Chartres:* "The great cathedrals after 1200 show economy, and sometimes worse. The world grew cheap, as worlds must" (1, p. 9). The topic of economy is only one manifestation, though an important one, since the Virgin's decline was partly due (according to Adams) to a disappointed bourgeoisie who withdrew their money from religious investments for more profitable ventures (13, p. 251). But taste in art followed the law as well. Stained glass showed a dramatic deterioration within fifty years, and even within a single structure like Chartres Cathedral the superiority of the old tower to the new bears witness, says Adams, to degeneration. What was true of architecture was, for him, true of all art (8, p. 141).

There is social degeneration in the book as well. Can the full values of medieval verse be recovered, and is not the stained glass of Chartres Cathedral beyond the aesthetic

---

[18] See Jordy, pp. 113–20, for the influence of Comte on the *History*. For his influence on the "Letter," see pp. 254–55.

apprehension of moderns? The narrator becomes weary and impatient with the necessity of having to write a book expounding the glory of Chartres instead of responding to it intuitively, and the very fact that it must be written, that this art must be explained, itself points to social entropy:

One loses temper in reasoning about what can only be felt, and what ought to be felt instantly, as it was in the twelfth century, even by the *truie qui file* and the *ane qui vielle* . . . . Still, it may be that not one tourist in a hundred—perhaps not one in a thousand of the English-speaking race—does feel it, or can feel it even when explained to him, for we have lost many senses. [8, pp. 128–29]

Most of all, woman has been degraded—a particularly ominous sign, since she more than man represents instinct, and the reader is expected to see in chapters like "The Three Queens" (11) and "Nicolette and Marion" (12) an ironic commentary on the modern position of woman. The same inexorable movement toward degradation underlies the final triad of chapters as well, for the temporary triumph of mysticism and its inevitable defeat by scholasticism signaled the decline of instinct, woman, and Virgin. These subtle equations, all linked together through a system of architectural analogies, are woven through the *Chartres,* creating a tightly knit world in which action on one plane necessarily possesses significance on all, and producing a vision of medieval instinct against which contemporary man is indeed a degraded and pitiful Gerontion.

It has already been observed how the travel book structure creates the sense of immediacy inspiring the narrator to those subjective responses forming a vital strategy of the book, elevating him to the position of the collective Western consciousness, allowing him to transform historical into aesthetic judgments, and compelling him to understand the forces behind the symbols of art. The framework also acts as the aesthetic matrix by which these effects are unified with the expressions of decline, some of which have been observed above. Even more, this framework is itself the literary expression of Adams's later view of historical entropy, synthesizing these random references to the decline of energy into an aesthetically satisfying unity and emphasizing the need for history conceived as a relation of force.

The very opening lines of the book, in the preface itself, are charged with significance. There Adams takes pains to substitute "niece" for "son" in the lines: "Who reads me when I am ashes,/Is my son in wishes" (p. xiii). The *Education* is addressed to young men seeking their way in the world. Not surprisingly, the *Chartres* is addressed to young women, partly because it is a book about women and their power, more because (within the light of equations between women and instinct) they better than men can respond to the feelings evoked, but especially because, as an educational tract of a different kind from its companion, it spells out to contemporary womanhood how low the mighty hath fallen.

But this is a light and jovial reminder of entropy, and the tour structure also serves as a serious reminder of an irrecoverable past when the instincts of man, because more powerful, not only were more receptive to the force behind art but, to turn the matter around, were instrumental as a force for great artistic creation. To see the tour structure as such, one must understand the book's double point of view. For medieval man the distinction between the Virgin as symbol and as reality lay in the difference between her iconographical representation and the literal belief in a heavenly Virgin with power to intercede for man and alter the operation of natural law. As narrator, Adams seeks this latter awareness; and for a moment he achieves it, for the chapters on Chartres Cathedral (5–10) move from a conception of her symbolic role to repeated assertions of the Virgin's living and autonomous presence. Perhaps Adams meant these repeated assertions to serve not merely to draw the reader into his web of illusion, but to display as well the tenuous faith of a narrator who protests too much. Whether or not he so intended, they produce this effect, for the illusion of a living and miraculous Virgin is fractured at the end of chapter 10, and in chapter 11 a modern analysis of the real force behind the symbol begins. The force is not a literal Virgin for the modern narrator, but the force of sex.

The framework's juxtaposition of the past and the present, with each era's respective views of the Virgin, produces three important effects. First, the juxtaposition itself becomes a literary expression of entropy, since the movement from a conception of a literal Virgin to a modern view of her as a symbolic projection of the sexual drive represents a movement away from emotional fervor in favor of rational analysis. As Blackmur observed, "When what has been felt as a primary force and cultivated as a symbol comes to be felt only as art and cultivated only as taste, then, by so much, have the values of life lost their edges in settling twilight."[19] Within the *Chartres* not only is that sense of loss evoked by the framework, but the framework itself is the literary equivalent of Adams's "scientific" law of social entropy.

The framework has an artistic use, as well as a "scientific." Through the framework the narrator was established as the collective consciousness of the West (he can only be this by beginning with the present and trying to recapture the past). All his statements about the medieval era are thus modified by his modernity, a fact apparent in the difficulty he has in achieving identification with the medieval spirit and in his penchant, seen in the last six chapters, for rational analysis of the medieval Virgin. Because of this double point of view the book characterizes the narrator just as much as he characterizes his subject. Thus all the

[19] "The Virgin and the Dynamo," p. 153.

various expressions of entropy within the book which were alluded to earlier are perfectly consistent with the narrator's modern character, which is defined through the framework.

Adams's experiment was triple-layered, with all the layers inextricably involved, so that the framework serves not only the purposes of science and art but those of history as well. Precisely because the framework creates the tensions of a double point of view, the modern and the medieval, both views converging within the mind of the narrator, it emphasizes the historical problem of relation which Adams had undertaken to solve, using himself as the constant within his experiment and, to repeat the words of the 1918 preface to the *Education*, assuming nothing "as true or untrue, except relation" (p. vii). The framework of the *Chartres* establishes that relation in history as a movement from the literal belief resulting from emotion to the empty understanding arrived at by rationality, and it poses this movement as a problem for scientists and historians. Even more important in terms of the experiment, the framework of the *Chartres* is indeed the very world of the *Education;* so that, in view of the identical persona operating within each book, the groundwork for the complementary nature of the books conceived of as literature, as "science," and as "history" is firmly established by this indispensable literary device.

The Theory of Unity and the Argument of the *Chartres*

In the *Education* Adams referred to college professors as a special breed. A prolonged stay in the academic world marked a man for the rest of his days. From the pages of "Failure," where he recounts his teaching experience at Harvard, one gathers that a teacher of history has no social utility and just one satisfaction—that he can educate himself, or at least try to, at the expense of his students. And that is his mark. He remains a perennial schoolboy.

Henry Adams was no exception. He too suffered from the occupational hazard. Although he dismissed his nine-volume *History* with an air of contempt in his later life, he remained forever a student of history; but his later years showed a lessening interest in the content of history and a growing obsession with history's meaning. He could not be satisfied with chronology or description so long as the possibility of a control explaining all of human development dazzled his thought. With aims so high, the manner of his expression and the problems attracting his mind naturally accommodated themselves to his professed goals. He needed a basic issue, a basic terminology which would have meaning within a variety of disciplines outside history, and this he found in the terms *unity* and *multiplicity*.

As Adams employed these terms, they took on a variety of colors and values, but always they had reference to the central problem of existence—for the individual, for humanity as a whole. It was the eternal problem of the one and the many. Unity is coherence which provides man with an explanation of his place in the universe; multiplicity is either meaninglessness or partial meaning, the explanation of man in relation to individual facets of experience, not in relation to an absolute. The issue has obvious relevance to other disciplines as well. For the artist, unity means the creation of a successful, organic work of art. For the theologian, it means a concept of God and the relationship man bears to God. For the scientist, it means some ultimate theory which can explain the operations of all phenomena. Of course for Adams it meant all these things and more, and so the underlying issue of the *Chartres* and the *Education* is breathtaking in its scope and complexity, and cosmic in its significance.

Precisely because of its manifold implications, Adams's concern with this issue has led to a view of him as a belated romantic. He wanted to know the explanation of everything, critics say, and since he dramatized his quest for an absolute, they picture him as a man in the throes of romantic agony. Blackmur rightly called his a mind destined to failure, even though in the grandest sense, because mind remains finite even in its quest for the infinite. But Baym, who used the epithet of "belated romantic," claimed that Adams regarded himself "as an Hamletesque figure." There is Adams's cosmic and poetic loneliness, and there is his notion of heroic failure to point to in support of the idea. And yet, though Baym controlled his description by insisting that the romantic image was a purely literary projection, it can nonetheless be a misleading notion.[20] Elements of this kind are certainly present in Adams's work, but similar elements appear in the work and thought of writers in all ages. Was Shakespeare an early romantic? Worse than confounding the tradition to which Adams belongs, this view tends to obscure the guiding impulse of his work.

His major purpose was to see if he could display a necessary sequence in human history. The Ara Coeli image which recurs hauntingly throughout the *Education* symbolized his continual quest for this end, and in "The Dynamo and the Virgin" he declared how he would attempt to find sequence:

He [Adams, the historian] cared little about his experiments and less about his statesmen, who seemed to him quite as ignorant as himself and, as a rule, no more honest; but he insisted on a relation of sequence, and if he could not reach it by one method, he would try as many methods as science knew. Satisfied that the sequence of men led to nothing and that the sequence of their society could lead no further, while the mere sequence of time was artificial, and the sequence of thought was chaos, he turned at last to the sequence of force. [25, p. 382]

[20] The reference to Blackmur is from "The Expense of Greatness: Three Emphases on Henry Adams," *Virginia Quarterly Review* 12 (July 1936): 404. See Max I. Baym, *The French Education of Henry Adams* (New York, 1951), pp. 209–26, for Adams as romantic failure. Baym recognizes the failure as a literary pose (pp. 217, 220, 225), but thinks of the pose as part of literary romanticism.

Adams's notion of force, needless to say, did not exclude the content of these other sequences—especially thought, whose movement vitally interested him. Rather, force became the common denominator of all things. Its movement allowed him to transform these other sequences into necessary ones, as *Mont-Saint-Michel and Chartres* demonstrates.

Subtitled "a Study of Thirteenth-Century Unity," the *Chartres* in fact spans three centuries, each marked by a different conception of unity. No doubt the reason for focusing upon the thirteenth century in the subtitle is that he thought of it as a critical point, when historical motion predicted the modern world. But in content the *Chartres* focuses upon the Medieval Transition (1150–1200). Transition implies movement, and to know its elements one must be aware of what came before and what followed; and so the book embraces three centuries. He called this transition a balance between thought and act (16, p. 385), an unstable equilibrium of the components of the eleventh century and the thirteenth. To show a sequence of forces merging smoothly into each other, as well as to create the illusion of unity artistically, he adopted the method of telescoping time, making each section of the work a display not merely of a single century but of the other two as well. Thus Mont-Saint-Michel, which primarily represents the eleventh century also contains the Merveille, which embodies the new spirit of succeeding ages since it spans the twelfth and early thirteenth centuries. The chapters on Chartres (5—10), the expository chapters on feminine power (11–13), and the concluding section on philosophy all shuttle across at least two centuries to create an important strategy. The technique renders the sequence of force which he followed in the *Education,* and it is intimately bound up with his "scientific" notions of unity. An analysis of the structure of the book will show the individual components within a larger sequence of force, then the means by which the book binds them together, and finally the way this structure reflects his theory.

The principal concern of the first three chapters is the eleventh century, and its guiding spirit is action unhindered by the complications of reason. The action is primarily military, but its goals are unity and are reflected in William's conquest of England and in the ardor of the First Crusade. Adams sees the political unity, either achieved or attempted, as a direct expression of a single unifying force. It seems to be no accident that the Trinity is no concern of Mont-Saint-Michel, and that the Virgin is bypassed, for both Trinity and Virgin dilute the conception of a single energy, God. He grounds this concern with unity in the historical environment. The Normans had the zeal of converts, having turned to Christianity from paganism with its multiplicity of gods only a little more than a century before William embarked on his conquest, and hence their major interest was the defense of monotheism; the defense, that is, of a unity uncomplicated by Trinitarian conceptions. A concern with this kind of unity is the major force of that age, a concern of feeling rather than thought, and even less of feeling than of action. Eleventh-century society is a direct and immediate expression of the primal, undivided energy of God. "We have little logic here, and simple faith, but we have energy" (1, p. 8). "One looks back on it all as a picture; a symbol of unity; an assertion of God and Man in a bolder, stronger, closer union than ever was expressed by other art" (3, p. 50).

There is good reason for Adams's reference to the Virgin as a great anarchist (13, p. 261). The transition of the twelfth century, characterized and defined in chapters 4–10, moves away from the immediacy of God's influence translated into direct act and depends for its unity upon the intercession of the Virgin. The force of the Virgin is human rather than divine, and its wellsprings are emotion and intuition rather than action. Humanity is a part of the multiplicity and irregularity created by man's free will with its apparent ability to contravene the divine. As such, man represents an incongruity within the rigorous harmony of the divine plan, and this is reflected in the peculiar unorthodoxies and structural deviations of Mary's cathedral. She subsumes both God and the Trinity; insofar as she does, the twelfth century is one step removed from eleventh-century immediacy. It is the difference between the direct apprehension of God as unity, translated forthrightly into action without intervening agency, and the indirect apprehension of him through the mediation of the Virgin, translated into art.

But through the Virgin one achieves unity nonetheless, for she harmonizes man's acts and divine law through an intuitive, nonrational assertion that such harmony does exist, although perhaps it is not susceptible of proof. Although the center of gravity has shifted—Michael represents man's championship of an assumed unity or God, the Virgin is a means of reaching toward God—instinct is not far removed from direct action; both are nonrational and require no reasonable proof of unity. Both exist as simple assertions of it.

The character of the thirteenth century is radically different. Abelard (14) is its harbinger and Thomas (16) its apotheosis. Through reason they seek God, though at first glance they seem to participate in the life of preceding centuries. The syllogism, like the Romanesque or Gothic cathedral, adopts the heavy architectural method of building toward God, using logical inference in place of granite or marble. But there is a significant difference. With the exception of Abelard's adversary, William of Champeaux, these philosophers do not assume God but seek to prove him. Thus the conclusion they seek to arrive at is actually the beginning point of eleventh-century action and twelfth-century intuition. The unconscious assumptions of an earlier time have moved into the consciousness to become the objects of rational analysis. Thomas is a forerunner of the world of the narrator.

But these three conceptions of the forces attaching man to God, of the forces providing unity within a universe, are

presented with a deliberate ambiguity. It is well to recall
the book's double perspective, touched upon earlier, because through it the sections of the book are bound tightly
together into the major argument of the *Chartres*. The
medieval point of view and that of the modern narrator are
presented concurrently, so that to modern eyes, the medieval
realities of God and Virgin appear as act and intuition, and
so that the presumed unity achieved by act, intuition, and
reason is seen as aesthetic rather than metaphysical unity.
The progress of the book, indeed, can be measured according to the emphasis given either point of view. In the first
ten chapters, the tour proper, the emphasis is upon medieval
conceptions of God and the Virgin as real forces. The narrator's point of view is subsidiary, contained within the
framework wherein he makes clear that he maintains an
aesthetic distance from Michael and the Virgin. Thereafter
the emphasis changes, but the last six chapters of the book
(11–16) are nonetheless united to the earlier part.

Chapters 11–13 form a single unit devoted to the reputa-
tions of historical women based on fact and legend (11), to
the position of women as they appear in the foremost poetry
of the time (12), and to the Virgin herself as she appeared
in legend (13). The section as a whole strikes an apparent
balance between medieval and modern views. On the one
hand, legend, poetry, and fact recreate medieval society as it
saw itself; on the other, these same elements act as inherent
commentaries upon the Virgin as a sexual and human force,
as opposed to a divine one.

"The Three Queens" (11) calls the reader's attention to
precisely this modern kind of equivalent. As noted earlier,
"The study of Our Lady, as shown by the art of Chartres,
leads directly back to Eve and lays bare the whole subject
of sex" (11, p. 196). The narrator pursues the matter by
quoting an authority on manners of the twelfth century, M.
Garreau, and by displaying the interpretations in art, made
by a twelfth-century poet, of the most fundamental issue of
Christendom: the Fall of Man. The "Mystery of Adam"

blames the fall on Eve's greater intelligence: "Eve was justly punished because she should have known better, while Adam, as the Devil truly said, was a dull animal, hardly worth the trouble of deceiving" (11, p. 204). But most important for his argument are the relationships created by the influence exercised by Eleanor of Guienne, Mary of Champagne, and Blanche of Castile: "We have only to notice the coincidence that while the Virgin was miraculously using the power of spiritual love to elevate and purify the people, Eleanor and her daughters were using the power of earthly love to discipline and refine the courts" (11, p. 211). In the poetry of courtly love the narrator finds aesthetic equivalents to the force behind Chartres Cathedral, and by the nature of the poetry, that force is expanded from the person of the Virgin to the power of sex.

The criticism of the poetry is much the same as the criticism of Chartres Cathedral, and this is the most basic way in which the section is drawn into relation with the tour in the first ten chapters. Christian of Troyes's artistic notions of religious mystery are "like that of the Gothic cathedral, illuminated by floods of light, and enlivened by rivers of colour" (11, p. 213). But most important for his aesthetic point of view, the narrator establishes within a single poem the same courteous tone of address directed to an earthly lady as is used in addressing the Virgin. Earthly love blends with heavenly, surely a commonplace observation on this kind of literature! Everyone knows that the age instinctively felt an opposition between sacred and profane love, and that the two could only be brought into harmony when the love of a lady could be seen as a symbol for the love of God or the Virgin. But Adams reversed this view, seeing in devotion to the Virgin the basic sexual drive. The reversal shows the distance between the modern and the medieval world. And the narrator's aesthetic equivalence between sexual and religious love, established in "The Three Queens," becomes predominantly a sexual analysis in the following chapter.

There he views "Li Gieus de Robin et de Marion" and

"Aucassins et Nicolette" as reflections of the superiority of women to men in the full range of medieval society, from peasant to noble. The woman in each case is the stronger force, in terms of both her emotional stability and her mental ingenuity. This exaltation of things feminine becomes apotheosized in the "Roman de la Rose," which embraces in its symbolism earthly feminine ideals that eventually culminate in the Virgin, all within the context of a Court of Love. The treatment of each story by the narrator is the really important element, however, for it supports the narrator's modern analytic view more than it does medieval religious views.

From the "Aucassins et Nicolette," the poem discussed at greatest length, the narrator quotes a long soliloquy in which Aucassins compares the joys of heaven to those of Nicolette, with the former found wanting (12, p. 231). Just as he did in his earlier analysis of the "Chanson de Roland," he finds religion a subsidiary factor. It colors society less than society colors it, giving it emphases and values to suit human needs even when these colors violate dogma. One way in which society colors it is shown in "Li Gieus." There Marion acts as a mother figure to the incompetent Robin, thus reenacting the role of the Virgin as she is defined in chapter 10 (p. 194). Even the "Roman" becomes an implicit commentary on the fictional Virgin, depriving her of reality. The narrator characterizes the Court of Love as a hiding place and refuge from the ugliness of the world: "The poet who approached the walls of the château and saw, outside, all the unpleasant facts of life conspicuously posted up, as though to shut them out of doors, hastened to ask for entrance, and, when once admitted, found a court of ideals. Their names matter little. In the mind of William of Lorris, every one would people his ideal world with whatever ideal figures pleased him" (12, p. 246). The chapter ends with the "Roman," and the reader recalls the end of the tour in chapter 10, "The Court of the Queen of Heaven." The two courts are equivalent. The Virgin's shrine served the same purposes as the Court of Love in the "Roman," and both possess the same reality, the appeal of wish fulfillment evoked by man's sexual adoration of women.

This analysis of the Virgin as sexuality, as earth mother, as a grand and heavenly wish-fulfiller, exists more by implication and analogy than through specific, detailed, cold exposition. The literature upon which Adams relies embodies situations whose elements are parallel to those found at Chartres, so the narrator can approach both architecture and literature with the same critical vocabulary, inferentially establishing equivalences on the way. But in "Les Miracles de Notre Dame" (13), analogy gives way to total identification between Virgin as symbol and the sexual forces which the narrator sees operating behind her—and this precisely because the body of literature discussed in the chapter focuses upon her alone. As such it validates the analysis implicit in chapters 11 and 12 and introduces a new element which cements the section firmly to the tour before, and to the book's theoretical conclusion.

Of the Virgin as mother figure, the story of the widow who stole the Christ from the icon of a Church madonna extends the vision of Mary found in chapter 10 (the tour's conclusion) and harmonizes with the conception of Marion as mother to her lover in chapter 12. For the Virgin as religious embodiment of sexual love, one need only refer to the knight whose tourney she fought, a favor for which she exacted his enduring loyalty as earthly lover. Her refining influences, her ability to invest the lowly and the naïve and the vulgar with an exalted dignity (the theme of chapter 11, where women's influence is so defined) concludes this chapter in the touching story of the tumbler who, consecrating his poor talent to Mary, strikes the uppermost ranges of emotion: "Lady, who never yet could blame / Those who serve you well and true, / All that I am, I am for you" (13, p. 280).

But the chapter also explains the irregularity and unorthodoxy of Mary's shrine at Chartres, and in so doing it
not only contributes to a fuller understanding of Mary's
character but prepares for the concluding chapters as well.
In the separation of the sexes Adams saw imaged the perennial problem of philosophy—either unity exists, or it does
not. Sexual differences suggest the latter, but sexual union,
with its production of children, implies the former. Sex
raises the question but answers it paradoxically. How fitting
that a sexual symbol should resolve the same problem—
unity or multiplicity—when it appears in a religious context.
Either the universe is rigorously controlled by God, in which
case man is united with God but has no freedom of will, or
man has free will, in which case God's universe is not truly
a unity. The Virgin allowed man to have it both ways (an
important issue in the concluding chapters) by acting as if
both views were true. The tale of the nun who abandoned
her religious calling to lead a life of sin, only to be saved by
the Virgin, exemplifies Mary's willingness to absolve humanity from the legitimate consequences of sinful action.
"This general rule of favour, apart from law, or the reverse
of law, was the mark of Mary's activity in human affairs"
(13, p. 261). Her behavior shows not capriciousness so much
as her belief that perhaps man does not have free will. God
created the world; He alone is responsible for sin—or at
least so this view of Mary would have her contend. "She
knew that the universe was as unintelligible to her, on any
theory of morals, as it was to her worshippers, and she felt,
like them, no sure conviction that it was any more intelligible
to the Creator of it" (13, p. 274). On the other hand, the
Virgin of these miracles can behave as if man did have free
will. She has her own dislikes as well as likes, and she rejects
those she dislikes with a firmness implying that their behavior is conscious, rational, and volitional. Such is the
moral of the story of the usurer and the widow. Her behavior explains the irregularity of her cathedral, where a

certain unorthodoxy creeps into and violates church tradition. And it foreshadows the failure of reason as a source for unity within the last chapters. Reason cannot solve the dilemma, God's will or man's, but intuition can by having it both ways. "If the Trinity was in its essence Unity, the Mother alone could represent whatever was not Unity; whatever was irregular, exceptional, outlawed; and this was the whole human race" (13, p. 261). By subsuming the Trinity, Mary linked these outlaws into an inextricable relationship with the unity of heaven. But it was a relationship based on intuition, a simple assertion of the feeling of unity rather than an objective assertion of the world as it is, and so it was bound to fail.

By this method, this use of poetry as an implicit commentary on the first ten chapters of the book as well as on the concluding triad of chapters, chapters 11–13 firmly cement the entire book into a single thematic structure. But the method goes beyond theme and reflects what Adams could later quite fairly think of as the "scientific" strategy of the *Chartres*. This analysis of chapters 11–13 has demonstrated a subtle progression toward modern analysis of the Virgin as a sexual figure rather than as the figure she represents to the true believer. In chapters 11 and 12 the Virgin's sexual meaning exists more by implication than direct identification, to repeat, but in 13 this meaning becomes entirely clear. What is most significant is that the progression takes place because the narrator implies correspondences between secular poetry and the religious figure of the Virgin in two basic ways: by having characterized the Virgin earlier in the narrative in such a way that the poetry and legends presented in 11–13 necessarily reflect upon the real forces behind her—the Virgin's unorthodox behavior in literature corresponding to the unorthodoxy of her cathedral, for example; and by applying the same critical terms to the poetry which were used with reference to the cathedrals (11, p. 213).

When one recalls the method of the first ten chapters, the

controlled associational method of the narrator, one realizes how the system of correspondences and equivalences in chapters 11–13 is a continuation of the earlier method. Now, precisely because the narrator once again is merging his subjective judgments with the "objective" elements of poetry and legend, the progression in chapters 11–13 toward a modern view of the Virgin takes on special significance in the light of Adams's "scientific" experiment. Adams, we recall, wanted to trace the movement of thought conceived of as force. The movement of his own thought, though apparently focusing upon legend and poetry, becomes increasingly analytic. Does this process itself not duplicate the unconscious movement of historical thought, the drift toward the rationalism of Saint Thomas in the final chapters, the drift toward reason without emotion in the pages of the *Education?* That at least is the question raised by the method and movement of these chapters, and merely by raising it Adams has satisfied the requirements of his "scientific" experiment. His own thought, at least, has so drifted. Whether or not the thought of man collectively follows the pattern is an affair for future scientists and historians.

One more observation must be made. Because Adams's analysis in these chapters emerges through implications to be drawn from rather beautiful, often tender legends and poetry, the reader himself is drawn into the trap, in this section more successfully than in the first part (1–10). Ironically, in the tour proper the narrator tries to make the Virgin come alive to the reader through architectural criticism; yet in this section (11–13), where the Virgin is being rationally analyzed as a sexual force, she seems more alive than ever because her humanity is revealed so beautifully by a poem like that of the tumbler and the Virgin (13, pp. 278–81) which concludes the section. And Adams the uncle rather slyly concludes this analytic section with a reference to feeling:

Beyond this we need not care to go. If you cannot feel the colour and quality—the union of naïveté and art, the refinement, the infinite delicacy and tenderness—of this little poem, then nothing will matter much to you; and if you can feel it, you can feel, without more assistance, the majesty of Chartres. [13, p. 281]

The trap has been sprung. All the while that the analysis of the Virgin as sexual figure has progressively grown stronger in chapters 11–13, the power of the poetry and the legends upon which the analysis depends has increased in direct proportion. The reader is disoriented by the discovery that, while his own emotions have been effectively engaged as they never were during the tour proper, where the narrator repeatedly insisted upon the Virgin's literal presence, his intellect at this precise moment now ironically tells him of her reality as myth.

One does not usually make references to private responses in order to analyze literature, but here it seems clear that Adams's statement at the conclusion of the section, "If you cannot feel [this poem] . . . then nothing will matter much to you," suggests that he has deliberately counted upon inducing a strong emotional response in the reader. And for what reasons? If the *Chartres* is a kind of tragedy, the failure of a culture, then reader engagement here emphasizes that tragedy. But Adams's motives are probably more complex than that because his art involved historical and "scientific" aims as well.

The study of relation is important to the latter aims, and by having the emotions jilted through reason, Adams can suggest powerfully to the reader that the movement of history indeed must be seen on this level, as a trend away from instinct and emotion and toward the dominance of rationality. But even more important, by inducing in the reader the same fractured sensibility possessed by the narrator, whose thought has inevitably moved, through the associational method, away from a tenuous faith in the Virgin toward rational analysis, Adams makes the reader personally validate the author's theory that thought possesses some kind of inevitable movement.

The question posed by the *Chartres* is this: Why did the Virgin, who occupied so much of man's talents and energies, disappear as an attraction during succeeding centuries? For the reader who has finished chapter 13, the question has become personal. And if the answer is not given, it is implied. Just as this poetry evoked emotional response in the reader, so too medieval man was strongly attached to the Virgin. But the reader's analytic faculties tear him away from his emotions and make him think of her, regretfully, as mythological only. So, too, medieval man found thought a compelling force destroying the Virgin. Indeed, the suggestion is that thought possesses an unalterable kind of movement. The associative method used by the uncle and the reader's own responses thus validate in literary terms a deterministic pattern for thought, for history itself. Perhaps this tactic of inducing a psychological response within the reader, though associated with Adams's "scientific" aim, is indeed his crowning artistic achievement.

The equilibrium between thought and emotion of chapters 11–13 marks the concluding chapters as well, although it appears in a somewhat altered fashion. Adams thought of the Transition as such an equilibrium, and this idea can be seen in the grouping of the chapters themselves—the dispute between William of Champeaux and Abelard (14), with the church's consequent silencing of Abelard representing late eleventh- and early twelfth-century subordination of reason to emotion; the Thomist synthesis (16) depicting the thirteenth-century triumph of reason; with the intervening chapter on the mystics (15) illustrating the transition in which reason and emotion are synthesized. The quality of this middle chapter, much the same as in 13, tenuously balances an appeal to emotion through the sermons of Saint Francis and the poetry of Adam of

Saint-Victor with an implicit analysis of the phenomenon described. Its substance duplicates the major theme of transition—"This paradox, that the French mystics were never mystical, runs through all our travels" (15, p. 329)—and Saint Francis is introduced as a figure to contrast with the more reasonable character of the French mystics and their Virgin.

The same equilibrium is recapitulated thematically in the other two chapters. Thus the conflict between nominalism, whose advocate is Abelard, and realism, championed by William of Champeaux, takes on the values inherent in the dual approaches to unity, by reason or by intuition. Abelard's nominalism insists upon proving unity and reemerges in the form of Thomism, whereas William's realism assumes the objective existence of God and bears a strong kinship to eleventh-century act and twelfth-century emotion; it is, in fact, the intellectual expression of these. Abelard's defeat at the hands of Bernard prepares for the short-lived Transition, followed by Thomism's approach to unity.[21]

In the last chapter the narrator's double perspective emerges in an ironically different way. Throughout he protests, "We study only his [Thomas's] art" (16, p. 361); the substance of Thomas's arguments is of less concern than its method. He admires in it the same qualities of structure exhibited in medieval architecture: "The essence of it— the despotic central idea—was that of organic unity both in the thought and the building" (16, pp. 374–75). In perceiving the art without accepting the reality of God as medieval man did, the narrator adopts the same stance taken

[21] Others have treated the relevance of the debate between nominalism and realism in greater detail and with varying emphases. See Levenson, pp. 278–88; Samuels, *The Major Phase,* pp. 291–305; Lyon, chapter 5. Samuels believes that Adams "learned to substitute 'science' " for philosophy (p. 305) and Lyon makes an equation between the Prime Motor and the dynamo.

earlier at the conclusion of the tour; but the aesthetic distance of these pages is more tragic, if less poignant, than when the narrator viewed the deserted cathedrals. They at least establish an organic unity of art which can exist independent of the validity of the God they seek to verify. But Adams sees Thomism as the ultimate expression of reason's search for unity. "From that time, the universe has steadily become more complex and less reducible to a central control" (16, p. 375). His aesthetic distance demonstrates the impossibility of accepting the validity of Thomas's thought and, by implication, the very concept of unity falters, if it depends for its existence upon reason. Thomas is its apotheosis and, for the narrator, Thomas fails.

Thus emerges the real argument of the *Chartres*. Unity can only exist when will (symbolized by Michael) and intuition (the Virgin) predominate over reason, for these former faculties assume its existence. But when reason emerges either to obscure or to obliterate these more primitive emotions, unity itself becomes a lost cause. By this point it is clearly a lost cause for the narrator, who next appears in the complex and disunified world of the *Education,* and these last chapters provide the transition between the earlier part of the *Chartres* and the *Education* itself. They provide an implicit commentary on all the basic issues—not so much of medieval life as of medieval life in juxtaposition to modern—which have been raised by the narrator's ambiguous perspective throughout the book. Abelard's nominalism coincides with the narrator's skepticism. Yet skepticism alone is not responsible for the demise of the medieval world picture. William of Champeaux's realism, the assumption of an objective God who is unity, was "the only possible foundation for any Church," (14, p. 297) and yet it, like nominalism, fatally led to pantheism. Reason contains internal contradictions which defy unity, at least in Christian terms, and the mystics, recognizing this, chose to reject reason itself rather than lose a world and a God. Thomas's ultimate triumph, on the other hand, implicitly led to the atrophy of sense which opens the book ("Our sense is partially atrophied from disuse" [1, p. 2]) and explains Adams's emphasis upon feeling. As narrator he is the end product of a Thomist world of reason, and because of it he experiences difficulty in recapturing the force of either Mont-Saint-Michel or Chartres.

Thomas leads forward to the *Education*. This is shown by the narrator, who early begins translating the snarls of medieval syllogistic thought into the snarls of scientific speculation. He begins the process with Abelard, comparing the debate over universals with the scientific debates of his contemporary world over whether unity exists in fact. (Recall Adams's letter to Taylor, in which he says that from the Prime Motor, he will work down to Karl Pearson, who claimed motion was the only unity.) But the process of intercalation, of translating faith into rays, so to speak, really gathers force in the final chapter. Throughout the exposition he shows that the problems Thomas wrestled with are the equivalents of modern scientific problems. And at every crucial point, every inch of the way, he discovers in Thomas's proofs mere inferences, unproved assumptions which science still wrestles with as problems. Thomas's proof of God thus becomes translated, in the language of mechanics, into a proof of the unity of energy; but whereas Thomas could not infer an infinite series of motors creating the energy, the narrator can, refusing to accept a unified source until it can be proved to exist: " 'we [moderns] can only say that we have not yet reduced all motion to one source or all energies to one law, much less to one act of creation, although we have tried our best' " (16, pp. 347–48). Thomas's Trinity becomes "more architectural than religious" in limiting God to three natures instead of to an infinity of them; his explanation of creation and the relation of the soul to individuality and matter become simplistic versions of the modern unsolved problem of mind and matter. But most important of all, Thomas apparently fails to provide man with a convincingly free will (16, pp. 368–71). God usurps man's freedom and opens the way for deterministic theories of man, theories of the kind which Adams himself sought to establish. Because Thomas could not reconcile man's freedom with God's, Henry Adams had to write the *Chartres* and the *Education.*

A rendering of Adams's "scientific" theory of history can enlighten the reader even further on the main argument of the *Chartres.* His "Letter to American Teachers of History" is a good guide at this point, for his "Rule of Phase Applied to History" contains a different facet of theory to be discussed later. The main axiom of the law of entropy upon which Adams grounds his thought is that all work (or, in history, all social movement) is accomplished through the conversion of one energy into another of lower intensity. The law, taken from mechanics, is extended by Adams to the vital processes—the energies released by plant and animal life, including man. Collectivizing the energy of individual men, he thinks of society as possessing a unified energy subject to the same laws.

This process of degradation actually began in prehistory, and became most marked toward the end of the Miocene period, when the luxuriant growth of vegetable and animal life appearing on the youthful planet began to disappear. Man's appearance upon the planet was late, not in its heyday but in its age, when vital energies had already declined.

Adams makes a rather vague distinction between force and energy, and he is not especially clear about the definition of either. He excused himself by observing that physicists themselves were not precise or in agreement as to their definitions, and he admitted in the *Education* that his theory "like most theories, begins by begging the question: it defines Progress as the development and economy of Forces. Further, it defines force as anything that does, or helps to do work" (30, p. 474). Apparently force is an abstract, collective term embracing the mechanical, vegetable, and animal worlds, whereas energy is used to define the specific variety of force exerted by anything, whether it be the sun or a man.[22] Adams's use of force corresponds to Schopenhauer's use of will, the basic motive power behind the universe—at least he identifies the two in the "Letter." He thinks of energy as individual expressions of that will.

Early man possessed to a high degree a total identification with this will. His acts were an absolute expression of it, much as the luxuriant vegetation of the Miocene was an expression of will or force potential. But as he continued in his growth, man naturally exhibited the same decreasing potentials within his personal energies as were occurring within the sum total of the universe of force at large. The total identification weakened, and he became a creature of instinct, one step removed from will. Instinct finally weakened and reason usurped its position.

Modern man is a creature of reason and reason's byproduct, thought, which is even further removed from force than instinct itself. And thought is degraded action. The man of instinct acts, the man of reason fails to act and transforms this failure into thought. According to this measure of value reason, and particularly superior mental endowment, is a marked sign of degeneration.

Reason and thought, in fact, are instruments for the degradation of force in nature, and Adams theorizes that they too operate according to the second law of thermodynamics. Man commonly thinks of his reason as an active agent, assimilating other forces and controlling them. He captures electricity through the dynamo, steam through the engine, and so forth. Adams reverses this ordinary view. He contends that man's thought is passive because it is attracted to these other energies, is captured by them. In

[22] In explaining Adams's theory, Donovan has made this distinction, p. 111.

this view, two things occur: first, the economies of force (dynamos and the like) invented by man dissipate the energies of the planet—coal power and electricity are consumed, for example. Second, thought itself is degraded in its energy potential. To show this Adams points to the position of man in industrial societies and reverses Marx's contention that idiocy is found only on the farms. In the interaction of thought and natural force, therefore, thought is dissipated. If natural force is infinite in its extent, and if man continues to be attracted to it, his reason will be dissipated long before the outside forces attracting it. Hence in the *Education* he predicts an ethereal phase when either thought must be exhausted, or the mind must make an ontological jump unprecedented in the history of the race.

Although the theory as here presented goes beyond the point of the *Chartres,* which stops with the ascendancy of man's reason, it does provide three important elements contributing to an analysis of the earlier work. First, it clarifies Adams's conception of unity, of which the book is a study. The conception is misleading. Medieval man's unity never existed as a cosmic reality, for the cosmos is a complex of shapeless and interlocking energies engaged in the process of lowering their intensities. Rather, unity was a subjective projection of man's deepest instinct. When instinct prevailed in man, when his energy potential was higher, he believed in unity; and the belief, springing from instinct, was transformed into act through art, social institutions, politics, and war. It was a higher energy potential which allowed medieval society to unite in religious belief, precisely because man acted on different precepts and with different faculties. The usurpation by reason was an expression of entropy. Reason cannot establish a metaphysical unity, nor, in a society guided by it, has it the power to unite society. Human institutions disintegrate, and the world of the *Education* emerges.

This concept of unity further explains the narrator's

double perspective throughout the book. He has stepped out of the pages of the *Education* armed with the power of reason, which both penetrates the real drives behind the unity of the *Chartres* and simultaneously, in its failure to believe in the Virgin, exposes his own degradation. But the drives which he perceives complete an understanding of the *Chartres* as an expression of entropy.

Although it has been observed that each section of the *Chartres* spans three centuries, each section is also predominantly concerned with one of them. The movement of the book from act through instinct to reason thus recapitulates the full development of the race as Adams viewed it in theory. The only point the critic must justify is the rapidity of the change. Surely evolution, even in reverse, did not occur with such speed. Man may be declining, but not quite so fast! There are two explanations for this difficulty. First, Adams was interested in relations between his day and the Middle Ages. Since his day was marked by reason and theirs by instinct, he chose quite obviously the era of transition between the two. The rapidity of deterioration he implies is thus illusory; it actually occurred slowly over the intervening centuries. Adams, that is, used the Medieval Transition as a metaphor to explain a movement which in reality had occurred over a long period of time, but whose elements of act, instinct, and reason all appear concentrated at the crucial moment of transition. Second, Adams was tracing the movement of thought, and after the Transition he found its movement unbelievably swift in its attraction away from theology toward science. He compared this movement to a comet, and the image is hardly extravagant, since modern science undeniably has separated at least the last two centuries irretrievably from all the rest of human history. Precisely because of the rapidity of the change, he believed that deterioration itself might work as fast. Indeed, the letters of his last years are a record of a man breathlessly awaiting the world's end.

The Theory of Phase and the Time Scheme of the *Chartres*

Of all the elements of Adams's artistry, the sense of movement which he creates in the pages of the *Chartres* is the
most accomplished and meaningful. This movement is a
function of the book's time scheme, which telescopes two,
three, or more centuries into a single unit through the
medium of the cathedrals themselves. After the completion
of the tour—which ends with chapter 10—Adams continues
to telescope time, using within each chapter a chronologi-
cal time scheme spanning at least two centuries, showing
in poetry, prose, and philosophy the basic unity of the period. This facet of the book has already been touched upon,
but lightly. Now its full significance can be appreciated.

Critics who have noticed this element have settled for
interpreting it as a device creating the illusion of unity by
establishing a delicate equilibrium in which time seems
arrested.[23] This interpretation seems fair enough, as far as
it goes, but in fact it does not go much further than the
direct statements Adams makes in the book, where he repeatedly exposes his hand by calling the Transition an
equilibrium. If this is all he had in mind, the time scheme
is a clever but rather obvious artifice.

In fact the device serves much larger purposes. Although
Adams called the *Chartres* a study of unity, the analysis of
that concept just concluded suggests that unity reduces itself
to the movement of forces; and the book would seem to
place at least as much emphasis upon motion as upon stasis.
To cite a passage mentioned earlier: "The nineteenth century moved fast and furious, so that one who moved in it

---

[23] Levenson (p. 239) says that Adams's aim is "to convert the tour
in space to a journey in time" and thus, by means of the cathedrals,
"simply watch the drama of the medieval imagination present itself."
Lyon observes that the fact that the cathedrals span the centuries has
much the same effect, the creation of an illusion of unity by creating a
stage upon which dramas can be enacted (chapter 5).

felt sometimes giddy, watching it spin; but the eleventh moved faster and more furiously still." (3, p. 32). Again: "Mont-Saint-Michel, better than any other spot in the world, keeps the architectural record of that ferment, much as the Sicilian temples keep the record of the similar outburst of Greek energy, art, poetry, and thought, fifteen hundred years before" (3, p. 32). This interest in motion links up with the most important motivation behind Adams's interest in history: the desire to show not sequence alone (for that would be mere chronology) but necessary sequence. This is the first function of the time scheme.

At this point the reader ought to recall how the narrator arrived at his conception of force—through subjectivity—so that art became its embodiment. Since this is so, the aesthetic relationships established among the elements of the cathedrals are an image of relationships of force, so that if the narrator establishes necessary aesthetic sequences, he has (according to the logic of his method) simultaneously established necessary sequences of force. In fact the book does this very thing, constantly shuttling back and forth between the centuries to emphasize motion and direction in artistic channels, in this way depicting the astonishingly rapid changes within the forces guiding social movement.

To establish the idea of necessity, the narrator makes repeated cross references to elements within Chartres Cathedral, even when the latter is not in his main line of vision. For example, he emphasizes the four triumphal piers and the four arches of the nave in the Abbey Church of Mont-Saint-Michel; but what do they support? (1, p. 7) Clearly not an eleventh-century church, since they are almost the sole remnants of that century at the Mount. The answer arrives by implication. They hold up the twelfth-century church of the Transition, of which Chartres Cathedral is the best representative. The Aquilon and Promenoir of the Mount are twelfth century, and the narrator relates them to the west porch of Chartres (3, pp. 35–36). The Salle des

Chevaliers and the refectory within the Merveille bring the narrator into the thirteenth century, and they are ante-chambers to the nave of Chartres (3, p. 40). Clearly Adams is building a theoretic church, a church of force, which depends upon equivalences like these for its construction, and by means of these equivalences he establishes necessary sequences.

Thus when the narrator-guide arrives at Chartres itself in chapter 5, "Towers and Portals," the cathedral has already become an image of forces spanning three centuries—eleventh, twelfth, and thirteenth—and he need only demonstrate how they unite aesthetically in Chartres in order to evoke the concept of an equilibrium of force, which is the Transition. Yet once the tour ends, the reader is conscious of a dissolution of aesthetic unity, partly because of the narrator's double perspective, partly because of a change in emphasis disturbing the elements held in aesthetic equilibrium. This changed emphasis appears particularly in the last three chapters of the book where, as was observed earlier, a recapitulation of three centuries of intellectual life diminishes the role of feeling and intensifies that of reason. But in the light of Adams's theory, this changed emphasis possesses a significance so far overlooked, and this significance is related to the second major purpose of the time scheme of the *Chartres*.

What attracted Adams in Willard Gibbs's theory of phase was that it provided, or seemed to provide, a method by which the phases of history postulated by Comte could be explained scientifically, and much of "The Rule of Phase Applied to History" is devoted to making Comte scientific. Where Comte found three phases, Adams named four: a religious, a mechanical, an electrical, and an ethereal—the last one being a period whose outward limit was highly speculative, perhaps to be reached by 1921, perhaps not till 2025, depending upon the dating of the beginning of the mechanical phase. The dating of these phases is approximate only, and is of less interest than the relations they bear to each other. Whereas Comte's phases were descriptive of the historical process, Adams, always seeking causation, found in the law of solutions a scientific hypothesis explaining historical change.

According to this law, any substance or combination of substances exists in a variety of equilibriums, or phases. Thus ice, water, and vapor are three phases of the same elements, H_2O. The observation was commonplace enough, but in view of the work being done by Gibbs, Rosenstiehl, and others, it took on compelling proportions. All matter, it appeared, could ultimately be reduced to motion. Let Adams speak for himself, for his earnestness is more convincing than a critic's exposition:

The solvent has been suggested or found for every form of matter, even the most subtle, until it trembles on the verge of the ether itself; and a by-stander, who is interested in watching the extension of this new synthesis, cannot help asking himself where it can find a limit. If every solid is soluble into a liquid, and every liquid into a gas, and every gas into corpuscles which vanish in an ocean of ether,—if nothing remains of energy itself except potential motion in absolute space,—where can science stop in the application of this fecund idea?[24]

Where scientists might stop was their own affair, but Henry Adams, for one, was not content to let their theories explain the mechanical world of physical force alone; and before long he made the leap—from matter as an energy to thought as an energy, subject to the same laws. What is history but the movement of thought passing from phase to phase? And just as pressure, temperature, and volume determine the critical point at which matter moves from one phase to another, so attraction, acceleration, and volume determine the shifts in the equilibrium of thought leading man from phase to phase in his historical experience.

[24] *Degradation*, p. 270.

Technically the *Chartres* is about a transition from pure
Romanesque to pure Gothic in architecture, but even the
superficial reader can tell that the Transition becomes a
metaphor for something more embracing. It has already
been observed that it operates as a metaphor for movement
from instinct to reason. With the "Rule" in mind, it is possible to go even further and see the architectural analogy as
a movement from the religious phase to the mechanical.

Several references in the book show Adams's conception
of the period as the last great flowering of a religious phase
of indefinitely long duration. The eleventh century thus is
characterized as a Christian continuation of a religious,
though pagan, past (1, p. 1), and the Virgin herself stands in
the line of Astarte, Isis, Demeter, and Aphrodite (11, p. 196).
Even the church as a conception is a sophistication of what
had existed since the dawn of remembered history: "The
choir was made not for the pilgrim but for the deity, and is
as old as Adam, or perhaps older; at all events old enough
to have existed in complete artistic and theological form,
with the whole mystery of the Trinity, the Mother and Child,
and even the Cross, thousands of years before Christ was
born" (10, p. 178). Thus on the one hand eleventh-century
Christianity is a mere variation of an ancient religious pattern; and on the other, the thirteenth century, exemplified
in Saint Thomas, is a harbinger of twentieth-century scientific modes of thought. Between the two lie the twelfth
century and Chartres Cathedral, a transitional church not
between Roman and Gothic alone but, in terms of phase,
between religious and mechanical.

One can go even further than this. Each phase, according
to the law of solvents, although composed of the same elements as the others, derives its character from a change in
their relationship. What played the role of a sun to satellite
planets in one phase itself becomes a planet, and a former
satellite moves to stage-center in the next phase. In the world
of the *Chartres* this image of interchangeable suns or centers

prevails and explains much that at first reading is confusing. It explains, for example, why Adams can speak of the thirteenth century in chapter 3 as characterized by the Virgin and by love ("The thirteenth century rarely let slip a chance to insist on this moral that love is law" [p. 43]) and nonetheless in the last chapter assign to this century the character of reason and intellect, the opposite of love and intuition. In fact both are true, depending upon which end of the spyglass of time one looks into. If one looks at the thirteenth century as the past—that is, in its relationship to the twentieth century—then reason is its center. But in chapter 3, Adams is looking forward; his base point is the eleventh century, and the thirteenth is the future. From this angle of vision, the high noon of the twelfth-century Virgin has become the brilliant afternoon sun of the thirteenth, with love still dominant even though reason is at its zenith.

The whole time scheme, then, is at once an image of shifting equilibriums and an image of a single phase, but a phase approaching its critical point when it will pass into another mode of being, and as such it reflects not merely a "scientific" truth but a highly sophisticated, viable conception of history. Adams belongs with Bergson and with T. S. Eliot in his assertion that history is man's experience of the world, and that the world as man sees and feels it at any given moment is a mélange of disordered and disparate elements which obtain their shape and meaning from the mind of a feeling, thinking participant. Traveling from the twentieth century back into the eleventh, and then moving forward again, the narrator sees time taking on different shapes, different relations, different values. It chiefly takes on the character of motion—a motion of millions of vibrating molecules of experience, often vibrating so closely that they appear as a solid, a moving body with definable characteristics. In *Mont-Saint-Michel and Chartres* each solid is nothing more than a myriad of impressions derived from fact, from fiction, from art, philosophy, and science. These impressions are solidified as symbols; Michael, who is act, the Virgin, who is love and intuition, Saint Thomas, who is reason. And these symbolic persons move—sometimes alone, sometimes in relation to each other. Michael moves fast in the eleventh century. In the twelfth, the Virgin appears, and she is moving very swiftly too—more swiftly than Michael, so that she appears to move into the future, and Michael appears to recede into the past; yet for a moment, as when one speeding train overtakes another, motion halts, or at least it seems to, and we are in the world of the Transition. Then Saint Thomas appears, and movement resumes. He too moves into the future, but at a far swifter speed than either Michael's or the Virgin's. It is the speed at which Adams must travel to reenter the twentieth century. By the time he arrives, he is ill, violently ill with vertigo: "Martyrs, murderers, Caesars, saints and assassins—half in glass and half in telegram; chaos of time, place, morals, forces and motive—" (*E*, 32, p. 471). But this is not the conclusion of the *Chartres;* it is, instead, the end of Henry Adams's journey as he describes it in the *Education,* and to it we must now turn.

3

The
Education
of
Henry
Adams:

The Creation
of a
World of Force

The Subjective Moments

The Education of Henry Adams is a strange book, a puzzling mixture of two modes of experience.[1] In the majority of episodes the persona Henry Adams, though involved, is also sufficiently detached to examine his world with apparent objectivity. But in a few episodes he is more personally involved and he responds in a more subjective way, as he does when he first goes to school, led by his awesome grandfather, or as he does when he witnesses his sister's death. Perhaps the clearest distinction between the two modes rests on the differing appeals which a variety of experiences hold for the persona. Generally, he seeks to impart meaning to the events of his life intellectually, but certain experiences do not appeal to the intellect. The reader of the book is struck, from the opening pages, by Adams's inclusion of sensory experience as a mode of education. His earliest steps in education are lessons of color and taste, "although one

[1] In his study of image patterns in the *Education,* Kenneth MacLean has similarly observed: "A distinguishing paradox of Western literature of recent time is the frequent combining, in even measures of poetry and prose, of the matters of society and history with those of personality and the individual. The *Education of Henry Adams* so combines." "Window and Cross in Henry Adams's *Education,*" *The University of Toronto Quarterly* 28 (July 1959): 332.

would rather suppose that the sense of pain would be first to educate" (1, p. 5). But this kind of experience confuses Adams, for he cannot understand its place within an orderly life; and the confusion continues throughout much of the book. In Antwerp he enjoys a lesson in art, "but it was education only sensual" (5, p. 74). Awakened to Beethoven and thrilled by picturesque Italy, he nonetheless complains that this experience is a dead end, distinguishing between two modes of education by declaring:

To young Adams this first plunge into Italy passed Beethoven as a piece of accidental education. Like music, it differed from other education in being, not a means of pursuing life, but one of the ends attained. Further, on these lines, one could not go. It had but one defect—that of attainment. [6, pp. 85–86]

Although he responds to the richness of aesthetic pleasures, he remains ignorant of their relative value in the total picture of education: "Exactly what they teach would puzzle a Berlin jurist" (6, p. 86). This appeal to the senses, for the most part, differentiates the subjective moments from the surrounding objective narrative, and the regularity with which they appear suggests that Adams, as author, attached to them a special importance. And it is likely that their meaning is to be discovered by thinking of them as a deliberate strategy connected with Adams's special motives for writing the book—his "scientific" and literary ends.

One of the most provocative statements Adams ever made about the *Education* appears in a letter to Margaret Chanler, in which he calls attention to an important idea:

I like best Bergson's frank surrender to the superiority of Instinct over Intellect. You know how I have preached that principle, and how I have studied the facts of it. In fact I wrote once a whole volume—called my *Education*— . . . in order to recall how Education may be shown to consist in following the intuitions of instinct.[2]

[2] 9 September 1909, Ford, 2: 524.

In his later essay, the "Letter to American Teachers of History," he pursues this theme by translating directly from Bergson's *L'Evolution Creatrice:*

"Consciousness, in man, is chiefly intelligence. It might have been, —it seems as though it ought to have been,—intuition too . . . . Another evolution might have led to a humanity still more intelligent, or more intuitive. In reality, in the humanity of which we make part, intuition is almost completely sacrificed to intelligence . . . . Intuition is still there, but vague, and especially discontinuous. It is a lamp, almost extinguished, which gains strength at long intervals, where a vital interest is at hazard, but only for a few instants. On our personality, on our liberty, on the place we occupy in nature as a whole, on our origin, and perhaps also on our destiny it casts a feeble and flickering light, but a light which pierces, none the less, the darkness of the night in which our intelligence leaves us."[3]

Two outstanding subjective moments within the *Education* clearly operate in this way to enlighten Adams—the scene on the Wenlock Edge of time in "Darwinism" and the death of his sister in "Chaos." But before these climactic moments Adams undergoes a series of subjective experiences which, if they do not illuminate the understanding of the young man groping for an education, do contribute to the reader's knowledge of the terms which successful education must encompass.

The process of Adams's education is the gradual isolation of sensory experience from intellectual. Quincy is a world of immediate sense perception, a world in which—as Bergson might contend—one *knows* rather than knows *about,* but succeeding experience obscures this kind of knowledge with the fog of intellect. Boston is the symbol of this denial— a denial of evil, of the religious instinct, of temperament itself—all of which Adams equates with the repression of instinct: "In the want of positive instincts, he drifted into

[3] *Degradation,* pp. 204–5.

the mental indolence of history" (2, p. 36). But later, when the boy travels south, his instincts are awakened in an important moment in which the moral evil of slavery, stimulating his New England conscience, is juxtaposed against the sensuous attractions of the scenery so as to revive in the boy an awareness of his fractured nature: "He had not a thought but repulsion for it; and yet the picture had another side" (3, p. 44), he observes, remembering that his nature is "half exotic" (1, p. 19). Hence he concludes: "He did not wholly come from Boston himself. Though Washington belonged to a different world, and the two worlds could not live together, he was not sure that he enjoyed the Boston world most" (3, p. 45). The boy's personal growth, then, recapitulates a split in force which can be observed on the national level, since slavery forebodes secession; and so he emerges as a microcosm of a larger narrative pattern of forces.

On his first trip abroad the elements composing the microcosm Henry Adams become more complex. The first subjective experience, in Antwerp, confronts the young man with what is obviously the religious past—an epoch symbolized by the cathedral and Rubens's "Descent from the Cross." The subtler artistry of the scene depends upon the carefully emphasized details composing it and Adams's reaction within that frame. The cathedral is a bridge spanning the medieval era and the Renaissance—both literally, since its construction began in the fourteenth century[4] (Adams mistakenly calls it a "thirteenth-century structure") and ended in the sixteenth century—and figuratively in its physical relationship to the town: "The thirteenth-century cathedral towered above a sixteenth-century mass of tiled roofs, ending abruptly in walls and a landscape that had not changed" (5, p. 74). Housed within is Rubens's seventeenth-century painting. In short, the same telescoping of time

[4] For some facts of the Antwerp Cathedral's construction, see Hugh Braun, *Historical Architecture:The Development of Structure and Design* (New York, 1959), p. 197.

used in the *Chartres* as a technique to signalize the concept of historical phase reappears, but here the young man's response to the scene is of special value, being personal rather than historical: "He was only too happy to feel himself kneeling at the foot of the Cross; he learned only to loathe the sordid necessity of getting up again, and going about his stupid business" (5, p. 74). As a subjective moment the scene is powerful. The very act of kneeling suggests lines of force pulling him asunder. The contrast between feeling and loathsome work recalls the polarities of Washington and Boston; but whereas there the conflict was symbolized spatially, here it assumes temporal dimensions. The young man now is torn between past and present and thus becomes a microcosm of the historical process itself, the past being defined as feeling, the present as its denial. Yet this is not all. Although Adams as persona calls the experience "education only sensual," the fact that his feeling has been directed to art elevates the original conflict between sense and intellect to an aesthetic level and foreshadows the very experience of translating art into force which links the *Education* to the *Chartres*.

The subject of Rubens's painting casts some light on Adams's awakening to Beethoven, his next subjective moment. "The Descent from the Cross" images the central belief uniting an entire culture; hence the belief once accepted by intellect could be fused with sense into the aesthetic experience of art. No such unity of human faculties exists within the modern world, however. The split in Adams, and by implication in all his contemporaries, is dramatized in the account of his sudden appreciation of Beethoven: "A prison-wall that barred his senses on one great side of life, suddenly fell" (5, p. 80). The wall imagery is important, for German life has been imaged in terms of enclosure, and the suggestion naturally follows that aesthetic experience can transcend such limitations. But the experience does not unite other realms:

His metaphysical sense did not spring into life, so that his mind could leap the bars of German expression into sympathy with the idealities of Kant and Hegel. Although he insisted that his faith in German thought and literature was exalted, he failed to approach German thought, and he shed never a tear of emotion over the pages of Goethe and Schiller. [5, p. 81]

Metaphysical unities could be no substitute for the synthesis provided by a religious orientation, and so his awakening aesthetic sensibilities remain isolated from the rest of his experience.

Rome, the city that symbolizes the center of Western culture, becomes the setting for Adams's next meaningful experience, and there he receives the impulse to explain the historical process, an impulse rendered through the familiar dichotomy:

To a young Bostonian, fresh from Germany, Rome seemed a pure emotion, quite free from economic or actual values, and he could not in reason or common sense foresee that it was mechanically piling up conundrum after conundrum in his educational path, which seemed unconnected but that he had got to connect. [6, p. 90]

The emphasis upon emotion as the equivalent of an older Rome is too pervasive not to be deliberate: "Italy was mostly an emotion and the emotion naturally centred in Rome." This Bostonian discovered "medieval Rome was alive; the shadows breathed and glowed, full of soft forms felt by lost senses. . . . Medieval Rome was sorcery" (pp. 89, 90). Hence the two falls which puzzle Adams—the demise of classical and of medieval culture—represent the decline of emotion and the objective correlation of that emotion, art, particularly the Church of Santa Maria di Ara Coeli, which later recurs as an image recalling Adams's search for sequence. These two, art and emotion, necessarily become the important keys to the solution of the puzzle which Adams mistakenly approaches through intellect.

His purpose can be seen in a previously quoted letter to A. S. Cook commenting on the *Chartres*. The opening remarks relate to the earlier volume: "I wanted to show the intensity of the vital energy of a given time." But the conclusion of the letter has reference to the *Education:*

> In other words, I am a creature of our poor old Calvinistic, St. Augustinian fathers, and am not afraid to carry out my logic to the rigorous end of regarding our present society, its ideals and purposes, as dregs and fragments of some primitive, essential instinct now nearly lost. If you are curious to see the theory stated as official instruction, you have only to look over Bergson's *Evolution Creatrice.* . . . The tendencies of thought in Europe seem to me very strongly that way.[5]

As persona, the young Henry Adams of the *Education* stands in pitiful contrast to the people who move across the pages of the *Chartres*. His sensory experiences confuse and puzzle him, whereas medieval man found in them a source of strength and unity.

Having allowed the reader to perceive the historical process in miniature through the subjectivity of his persona, Adams confirms the fracturing of historical force and personal sensibility in a pivotal chapter, "Treason" (7), in which the rupture in national forces leading to Civil War is paralleled by a similar rupture in Adams's social relations. In the eyes of the youth, Sumner's behavior in abandoning the cause of union because of his disgust with the South yields the somewhat sententious moral, "the rule that a friend in power is a friend lost" (7, p. 108). But the dramatic significance of the scene, evoked by the powerful terms attending it, clearly goes beyond mere homily. With Senator Sumner "the young man's education began; there it ended" (7, p. 107). From Senator Sumner he learned that "the profoundest lessons are not the lessons of reason; they are sudden strains that permanently warp the mind" (p. 108). Not

---

[5] 6 August 1910, Ford, 2: 546–47.

even Robert E. Lee's defection "cost young Adams a personal pang; but Sumner's struck home" (p. 108). Sumner represents the split between head and heart, the conflict between political interest and natural affection; and his course of action images the dichotomy in the boy's nature in a specially painful way. Earlier, Adams had renounced moral considerations to favor Sumner's election to the Senate (3, pp. 49–50); now he discovers that Sumner rejects the friendship of the Adamses because they moderate their antislavery stand to support the moral cause of union—at least as the pages of the *Education* present the issue.[6] Thus the treason of this chapter has both a political significance and a personal one for Adams the microcosm. The blind forces afflicting the nation with sectional strife affect his personal life as well, making of him the manikin whose sole reason for existence is the study of relation.

The meeting with Swinburne—overwhelming because his "quality of genius was an education almost ultimate, for one touched there the limits of the human mind on that side" (9, p. 142)—acts as a norm on the personal level of Adams's problem. Swinburne renews his awareness of the "dullness of his senses and instincts" (p. 142). Although he might never achieve the heights of sensitivity to which this poet rises (the scene has its obvious comic ironies), he might attain the perfect synthesis of intellect and emotion which the poet represents. But one just does not solve such a problem overnight, and Adams's dilemma is complicated by the historical dimensions it has assumed. In the next important scene at Wenlock Abbey (15, pp. 228–31), however, he goes a long way toward solving both aspects of the problem.

This experience, occurring "on the Wenlock Edge of

[6] For a fuller treatment of the background which led to a rupture in relations between Sumner and the Adamses, see Samuels, *The Young Henry Adams,* pp. 79–90. See also David Donald, *Charles Sumner and the Coming of the Civil War* (New York, 1960), pp. 373–81. Donald's account is more sympathetic to Sumner than Henry Adams's might be.

time" (p. 229), is climactic because it recalls the strands of previous subjective experience. First the contrast between subjective and intellectual modes of cognition appears, more clearly than in any previous scene, through the narrative framework in which the moment of apprehension occurs. It is a framework of intellectual speculation on the validity of Darwinism and Lyell's theories of geological uniformity as viable constructs for explaining man and his place in the material universe. As such these theories expand the historical problem to its greatest dimensions, placing Adams in a relationship not merely to the medieval world of Antwerp and Rome but to the beginnings of all life, symbolized by *Pteraspis,* the ganoid fish appearing as a fully developed vertebrate in the Silurian period of geological time. The narrative repeatedly emphasizes the concept of his personal relationship with the prehistoric past: "That here, on the Wenlock Edge of time, a young American . . . should find a legitimate parentage as modern as though just caught in the Severn below, astonished him. . . . To an American in search of a father, it mattered nothing whether the father breathed through lungs, or walked on fins, or on feet" (15, p. 229). "That *Pteraspis* and shark were his cousins, great-uncles, or grandfathers, in no way troubled him, but that either or both of them should be older than evolution itself seemed to him perplexing" (p. 230).

The problem of sequence in history once again focuses upon the persona. But for the young Adams, the intellect fails to provide relationship between him and *Pteraspis* precisely because evolutionary theories fail to prove a progression, a relationship of cause and effect operating logically from the beginnings of time down to the moment of his own existence at this center, Wenlock, where all time merges:

The vertebrate began in the Ludlow shale, as complete as Adams himself—in some respects more so—at the top of the column of organic evolution: and geology offered no sort of proof that he had ever been anything else. Ponder over it as he might, Adams could see nothing in the theory of Sir Charles but pure inference, precisely like the inference of Paley, that, if one found a watch, one inferred a maker. [15, p. 230]

Wedged into this framework appears the subjective experience itself, initiated by sensuous reference to nature recalling the immediate sense perceptions of Quincy and of Washington:

Perhaps he liked best to ramble over the Edge on a summer afternoon and look across the Marches to the mountains of Wales. The peculiar flavor of the scenery has something to do with absence of evolution; it was better marked in Egypt: it was felt wherever time-sequences became interchangeable. One's instinct abhors time. [15, p. 228]

With this reference to instinct, the moment begins in which all time sequences interchange (15, pp. 228–29), thus climaxing the telescopic technique which marks both the *Chartres* and the *Education* throughout.

The result of the experience has two vital facets. First, dynamic and temporal values are substituted for traditional static ones. It must be remembered that Adams has not abolished time but rather perceives its essence as change and motion (15, p. 231), a perception directly contradicting traditional concepts of time in which all movement is seen as leading to some predefined end. The traditional notion accepts time sequences but defines their operation within an enclosure of beginning and end, moving from a fixed past to a fixed future. The notion is embodied in Christianity, with its concept of a garden and a second coming; Adams sees Darwinism as an attempted substitute for religion, replacing the garden with *Pteraspis* and the second coming with the final perfectibility of man: "It was a form of religious hope; a promise of ultimate perfection" (p. 231). For Adams, on the other hand, the essence of time lies in its perpetuity as change and motion.

The second vital facet is that time's movement is centered

in the individual, who perceives through instinct this eternal flux of change and motion. The individual as center is stressed throughout the scene. "What *he* valued most was Motion, and . . . what attracted *his* mind was Change" (p. 231, italics mine). "Henry Adams was the first in an infinite series to discover and admit to himself that he really did not care whether truth was, or was not, true" (pp. 231–32). The scene thus climaxes the movement in which the persona emerges as a microcosm of the historical continuum. Here Henry Adams becomes the image of time itself, whose movement resists all human attempts to freeze it by giving it a pattern and meaning which man calls truth. All past time merges, undifferentiated, in him, and yet there is a disparate element within this meaningful experience. The shepherds of Caractacus or Offa "would have seen little to surprise them in the modern landscape unless it were the steam of a distant railway" (p. 229). "Coal-power alone asserted evolution—of power—and only by violence could be forced to assert selection of type" (pp. 230–31).

Later in the narrative, when Adams at Chicago finds himself thrown off balance by the dynamos which broke the unity of natural force, he stops for a moment to expostulate: "Did he himself quite know what he meant? Certainly not! If he had known enough to state his problem, his education would have been complete at once" (22, p. 343). The same thing might be said here to explain Adams's acceptance of Darwinism in defiance of instinct; he is frightened by the implications of an experience which he does not fully understand but which apparently denies the unity which he pursues. He has observed mechanical force in the guise of the railroad; but how this force relates to the thirteenth-century abbey nearby he cannot yet know, although Adams as artist deftly intrudes these vital elements which his persona must later measure (and, by implication, which only an individual mind reacting to force can measure).

Thus the persona has telescoped time through the

medium of the self, but he has not yet arrived at the sophistication of the Conservative Christian Anarchist who can
hold aesthetic and scientific motives together to effect an
individual unity of personal and historical experience when
all other modes fail. Quite the reverse! His newly found
conception of time as a continuum of motion and change
implies anarchy, and the possibilities of its composing a
unity within the sentient personality—a unity which he
achieves later in the role of Conservative Christian Anarchist—Adams rejects as the speculations of psychology: "Psychology was to him a new study, and a dark corner of education" (15, p. 231). "He put psychology under lock and key;
he insisted on maintaining his absolute standards; on aiming
at ultimate Unity" (p. 232).

Taking the path of intellect, then, Adams tries Darwinism
as a faith yielding total unity only to discover, on his return
to America, that Grant's administration repudiated all the
social implications of that faith. Intellect fails. But in the
next scene, the death of his sister at Bagni di Lucca, sense
also fails to provide coherence in experience. The moment
recalls his delightful apprehension of natural phenomena
earlier in Italy, and yet still earlier in childhood, at Quincy
and at Washington; but a powerful change occurs as he
penetrates nature's stage setting:

> Impressions like these are not reasoned or catalogued in the
> mind; they are felt as part of violent emotion; and the mind that
> feels them is a different one from that which reasons; it is thought
> of a different power and a different person. The first serious con-
> sciousness of Nature's gesture—her attitude towards life—took
> form then as a phantasm, a nightmare, an insanity of force. For
> the first time, the stage-scenery of the senses collapsed; the human
> mind felt itself stripped naked, vibrating in a void of shapeless
> energies, with resistless mass, colliding, crushing, wasting, and
> destroying what these same energies had created and labored from
> eternity to perfect. [19, p. 288]

What Adams perceives, then, is a "chaos of anarchic and

purposeless forces" operating behind all nature and leading man to ultimate extinction; but if the experience destroys even sensory unity, it teaches him the value of the senses: "He did not yet know it, and he was twenty years in finding it out; but he had need of all the beauty of the Lake below and of the Alps above, to restore the finite to its place" (p. 289). In the abyss of meaninglessness, he yet will find in the experience the meaning and value of "education only sensual," for through the aesthetic faculty man can order his life into a meaningful pattern.

By the time Henry Adams perceives chaos both sense and intellect have failed to provide coherence for him. Intellect's adherence to social Darwinism cannot achieve reform in American political life. And weakened aesthetic faculties, whose partial awakening either leads him to a dead past or confuses him in a shapeless present, fail completely at his sister's death. The memory of that death later teaches him the value of artificial form in an apparently chaotic world, but he never abandons intellect. In this connection his meeting with the geologist Clarence King is especially important.

It is the last subjective moment, and it occurs in "Failure" (20), the chapter following "Chaos." The description of this meeting amid the natural wonders of Estes Park (pp. 310–11) recalls both the values of nature allied with Quincy and Washington—the delight in pure sense perception, and the values of "Chaos"—the horror of anarchic force. Adams must bring the two motives into alignment, and King's scientific bias portends the synthesis of sense and intellect, of aesthetics and science, which is the subject of the book thereafter.

Most important of all, because these subjective moments have elevated Adams as persona into a microcosm of the historical process as it manifests itself both in the past and in the immediate present, the meeting with King suggests the very experiment of bringing "scientific" motives into alignment with literary ones in the *Chartres-Education* unit itself. In this connection the subjective moments, by making him a microcosm, have simultaneously established the persona as a manikin for the study of relation. The broader narrative pattern of the *Education*, its objective part which concerns social and historical matters, displays the forces which direct his path through the modern world.

The Pattern of Force and the Manikin's First Education (Chapters 1–7)

Throughout the first twenty chapters of *The Education of Henry Adams* there is a deliberate contrast between a narrative structure implying a world of force and an ignorant persona helplessly controlled by its impersonal operations. As the passive recipient of experience, the young Adams follows two major paths of education through "Failure" (20), and each ends disastrously. The first culminates in the Civil War ("Treason," 7); the second begins with his stay abroad during that war as private secretary to his father, the American minister to England, and it too ends disastrously with his attempt at reform in Washington during the postwar years. The disaster of his first education is presented as more a public than a private affair, for in this sequence of experience he has not yet reached the age when a man becomes aware of his powers and consciously attempts to exert them in the world. This first strand of education therefore creates the pattern of force which will control and finally overpower the manikin Henry Adams in his second education.

No commentator can fail to observe the rich dichotomies with which Adams paints his early life in Quincy, but it is a mistake simply to generalize this experience into the symbol of the child's identification with the multiplicity of nature, a Wordsworthian bond later disappearing in the sterile conformity which society demands of the child. This kind of reference certainly exists, but Adams is more interested in its operation within a unique historical context than merely in the general experience of the race. "No such accident had ever happened before in human experience," he writes tellingly. "For him, alone, the old universe was thrown into the ash-heap and a new one created" (1, p. 5). He emphasizes the novelty of his world with references to the mechanical age of railroad and telegraph and through repeated assertion: "The game was to be one of which neither he nor any one else back to the beginning of time knew the rules or the risks or the stakes" (p. 4). "All experience since the creation of man," so goes this theme of cosmic change, "all divine revelation or human science, conspired to deceive and betray a twelve-year-old boy" (p. 33). Like the times, the boy too is unique. Even though an Everyman, he is still highly individualized, branded as if he were Israel Cohen "born in Jerusalem under the shadow of the Temple" (p. 3) and, through the agency of scarlet fever, so affected physically and temperamentally that he became an exaggerated New Englander: "His brothers were the type; he was the variation" (p. 6).

This uniqueness of persona and culture acquires special meaning within the broader frame of reference defining the symbolism of Quincy. First and foremost "eighteenth-century" (1, p. 11), Quincy is also "colonial" (p. 7), even "troglodytic" (p. 3), the setting for the boy's "prehistoric stage of education" (p. 20) where he observes "the back of the President's bald head, as he sat in his pew on Sundays, in line with that of President Quincy . . . and had sat there, or in some equivalent dignity, since the time of St. Augustine, if not since the glacial epoch" (p. 15). This technique of telescoping time through frequent allusions to the historic and prehistoric past extends the values of Quincy beyond the eighteenth century into a broad and single continuum in human history, of which Quincy represents the final term whose individuation is Henry Adams.

A previous critic has noted that casual references through-

out the first chapter construct an unmistakable biblical context to support this reading.[7] From the first allusion to Israel
Cohen (1, p. 3), Adams participates in the symbolism of the
wandering Jew—a function which his role as sojourner
reinforces—and the identification suggests the ancient and
perennial character of the world to which he owes allegiance. The story of his education, he contends, is as old as
Cain and Abel. Quincy is a kind of Eden wherein Grandmother Louisa assumes the values of Eve, seducing the boy
into "rebellions against law and discipline," disseminating
"the seeds of the primal sin, the fall from grace, the curse of
Abel" (p. 19). Like Eden, Quincy has its garden, for "the
President rode the hobby of tree-culture" (p. 14), and the
boy's grandfather plays the role of Raphael in expelling him
from Eden by forcing him to school, thus suggesting, "Even
there the curse of Cain set its mark" (p. 12). "Quincy was
not a bed of thornless roses" (p. 11).

All these allusions to the Fall support the expansive symbolism of Quincy as a microcosm of traditional Western
culture, and Adams's career at first sight follows the pattern
of the archetypal Everyman expelled from Eden to face a
postlapsarian world. But this boy is the variation, not the
type; and Quincy appears on the brink of a dramatic rupture
in historical sequence; so the fall of Adams is not the general
Fall of Adam in which all men share and whose patterns of
experience all men repeat. Rather, the Fall here is used
ironically to represent the demise of a world structure cen-
tering about that myth, with the consequent need of a new

[7] In his Wisconsin dissertation Lyon has used the Fall construct,
which he observes in these early pages of the *Education,* as a basic
pattern of failure (chapter 6). Both Lyon and R. P. Blackmur, "Adams
Goes to School," *Kenyon Review* 46 (1955): 597–623 have treated the
symbolism of place in these early chapters, Lyon in terms of alternating
unity and multiplicity symbols, Blackmur in terms of imagination
(Quincy) and reason (Boston). Blackmur feels that Adams's education
abroad was not guided by either intellect or emotion but by gravitation, and hence his education was a failure.

terminology to give form to experience: "No one suggested at that time a doubt whether a system of society which had lasted since Adam would outlast one Adams more" (1, p. 16). The education of Adams as persona consists of the search for an alternative explanation—what Adams calls his quest after unity—and leads to the theory of history concluding the book; but although Adams as persona arrives at this theory late, Adams as artist structures the narrative according to its precepts from the opening pages of the *Education*. Read against the background of theory, Quincy represents the last throes of a religious phase in history which had begun its decline at the Renaissance and whose death is foretold by the important symbol of the railroad, which serves throughout as a measure of the growing strength of the mechanical phase as it destroys the remnants of the preceding religious phase.

If Quincy is the last reminder of a religious phase in history, the dichotomies of chapter 1 take on a greater significance, representing not merely the natural relationship of the child to nature before artificial standards of society are imposed but also, and more importantly, symbolizing a perennial mode of vision within Western culture itself. Connected with the theme of resistance, they provide the boy with a moral view of life, the traditional opposition between good and evil here supported by nature's dichotomies:

Resistance to something was the law of New England nature; the boy looked out on the world with the instinct of resistance; for numberless generations his predecessors had viewed the world chiefly as a thing to be reformed, filled with evil forces to be abolished . . . . The chief charm of New England was harshness of contrasts and extremes of sensibility—a cold that froze the blood, and a heat that boiled it . . . ; the charm was a true and natural child of the soil, not a cultivated weed of the ancients. The violence of the contrast was real and made the strongest motive of education. The double exterior nature gave life its relative values. [1, p. 7]

Thus the apparent dichotomy of Adams's Quincy childhood does possess a kind of unity—the traditional war of good and evil united by the balance of opposites; united still, indeed, within a Christian theistic framework. In later chapters of the book this meaning for eighteenth-century Quincy is sustained. Thus Adams claims that his persona "inherited dogma and *a priori* thought from the beginning of time" (2, p. 26). And after the Civil War, which obliterates the values of Quincy completely, the persona Henry Adams expostulates against Grant's administration in terms implying his inbred Quincy values: "The moral law had expired—like the Constitution" (18, p. 280). "The system of 1789 had broken down, and with it the eighteenth-century fabric of *a priori,* or moral, principles" (pp. 280–81).

Quincy's unity, however, is quite different from the unity portrayed in the world of the *Chartres,* and the distinction between the two worlds is vital to an understanding of the narrative pattern in the early part of the *Education.* In the medieval world, irregularities of form in a cathedral could be resolved by the Virgin's character, which saw good and evil not as polar opposites but as tonalities subtly merging one into the other. She could save an errant nun from damnation, despite the nun's sexual laxity (*C,* 13, p. 257); and if she could do this, she could quite consistently demand irregularities in her cathedral, as she did in the construction of the apse (*C,* 7, pp. 121–22), without sacrificing unity of form. Indeed, even the political dissension of her age, exemplified in the conflict between Pierre de Dreux and Blanche of Castile, was resolved in her cathedral through the harmonies of color in those disputants' respective windows (*C,* 10, p. 183).

In the world portrayed in the early pages of the *Education,* attitudes differ sharply. When the boy Adams first travels south, he displays a New England conscience which cannot tolerate irregularity of form. The road to Mount Vernon is rough:

To the New England mind, roads, school, clothes, and a clean face were connected as part of the law of order or divine system. Bad roads meant bad morals. [3, p. 47]

This emphasis upon order springs from a belief that good and evil are irreconcilable, a contrast arising from the New England climate familiar since childhood to Henry Adams:

After a January blizzard, the boy who could look with pleasure into the violent snow-glare of the cold white sunshine, with its intense light and shade, scarcely knew what was meant by tone. [1, p. 9]

Thus the order of New England is quite different from that of the medieval order, for the latter embraces irregularities which shock the Puritan taste. Indeed, New England's order is more apparent than real. Adams later made explicit in his "Letter to American Teachers of History" a concept which guides the structure of the narrative. He tried to reconcile apparent historical progress, which tended to support a Darwinian view of history, with his own degradationist convictions:

The degradationist can so far ameliorate the immediate rigor of his law as to admit that degradation of energy may create, or convey, an impression of progress and gain; but if the evolutionist presses the inquiry further . . . the degradationist replies, quite candidly and honestly, that this impression of gain is derived from an impression of Order due to the levelling of energies; but that the impression of Order is an illusion consequent on the dissolution of the higher Order which had supplied, by lowering its inequalities, all the useful energies that caused progress. . . .

"Thus Order in the material universe would be the mark of utility and the measure of value; and this Order, far from being spontaneous, would tend constantly to destroy itself. Yet the Disorder towards which a collection of molecules moves, is in no respect the initial chaos rich in differences and inequalities that generate useful energies; on the contrary it is the average mean of equality and homogeneity in absolute want of coordination."[8]

[8] *Degradation,* pp. 256–57.

This concept of a leveling of energies with a resulting appearance of order is the structuring principle of the early chapters in the *Education*. The unity of the *Chartres*, composed of a synthesis of rich irregularities that harmonize tonally, has degenerated in Quincy, the sole reminder of a religious phase in history, into a unity composed only of sharply contrasting opposites.

The collapse of this phase is foreshadowed by the death of John Quincy Adams, "when the eighteenth century, as an actual and living companion, vanished" (1, p. 20), and is symbolized in Boston by its individual citizens and by the character of society at large. Henry's father, Charles Francis, "possessed the only perfectly balanced mind that ever existed in the name," a "balance of mind and temper," an "unusual poise of judgment and temper" which was a model within its range (2, p. 27). The political expression of the father's balance takes the form of the Free Soil Party, whose three leading constituents all possess this same kind of poise. The theme of balance suggests a unity of personality, but this unity too is clearly an illusion.

As it affects Charles Francis, "such perfect poise—such intuitive self-adjustment—was not maintained by nature without sacrifice of the qualities which would have upset it" (2, p. 28). As was true of his father, so also Palfrey, Dana, and Sumner have renounced the affections—their basic desires and ambitions—to follow their careers in Boston. Paralleling this renunciation of the affections is Boston's loss of the religious instinct, expressed in the pulpit and in the naïveté of transcendentalism by an optimism totally denying the principle of evil. "The children reached manhood without knowing religion, and with the certainty that dogma, metaphysics, and abstract philosophy were not worth knowing" (2, p. 35), for "Boston had solved the universe" (p. 34) through an unwavering confidence in the powers of suffrage, free schools, and a free press. The simple dichotomies of Quincy have degenerated further in Boston into a truncated society without a knowledge either of emotion or of what is here considered its natural corollary, evil. The unity of Boston is an illusion consequent upon the sacrifice of the polarities of emotion and intellect, evil and good, by eliminating emotion and evil—surpassing even Quincy in its movement away from a medieval synthesis—Quincy at least had balance. But a mechanical phase of history, symbolized by Boston's State Street, whose moneyed interests will support the growing power of the railroads, unfeelingly equates capitalism with absolute good.

The disintegration of the already weakened unity of Quincy appears most forcefully within a political structure which, loosely held together by the concepts of Boston Brahminism, has dissolved into the secessionism of Garrison, Phillips, and Parker; the strict party discipline of Webster, Everett, and Seward; and the moderate Free Soilers led by Charles Francis Adams and Sumner. The splintering suggests the view of society in its breakdown described by Gustave Le Bon, whom Adams quoted in the "Letter":

"That which formed a people, a unity, a block, ends by becoming an agglomeration of individuals without cohesion, still held together for a time by its traditions and institutions."[9]

Like Boston, Washington also must be measured by Quincy standards to evaluate its disintegration; and the symbol of Mount Vernon takes on special significance in this connection:

Mount Vernon always remained where it was, with no practicable road to reach it; and yet, when he got there, Mount Vernon was only Quincy in a Southern setting. No doubt it was much more charming, but it was the same eighteenth-century, the same old furniture, the same old patriot, and the same old President. [3, p. 48]

This equation strikes the standard for comparison, and the

[9] Ibid., p. 252.

national capital emerges as the face of a coin whose reverse side bears the image of Boston. As a symbol of the South, the city of Washington creates its own unity proceeding from emotion and temperament, and it is this appeal which the young Adams senses instinctively on his visit there:

Slavery struck him in the face; it was a nightmare; a horror; a crime; the sum of all wickedness! . . . He had not a thought but repulsion for it; and yet the picture had another side. The May sunshine and shadow had something to do with it; the thickness of foliage and the heavy smells had more; the sense of atmosphere, almost new, had perhaps as much again . . . . The want of barriers, of pavements, of forms; the looseness, the laziness; the indolent Southern drawl; the pigs in the streets; the negro babies and their mothers with bandanas; the freedom, openness, swagger, of nature and man, soothed his Johnson blood. [His paternal grandmother was never a true New Englander.] Most boys would have felt it in the same way, but with him the feeling caught on to an inheritance. [3, pp. 44–45]

The South has rejected intellect for emotion and in this way can absorb the moral contradiction of slavery. What remains uppermost in the boy's mind, however, is the contradiction between George Washington and slavery: "He never thought to ask himself or his father how to deal with the moral problem that deduced George Washington from the sum of all wickedness" (3, p. 48). In the equation of Mount Vernon with Quincy, the narrative supplies the answer which the boy fails to get. Boston has sacrificed one pole and the South has sacrificed the other pole of a moral universe unified in Quincy.

Within these terms, therefore, Washington and Boston appear as contrary degradations of Quincy, though this regional polarity is still held in a tentative equilibrium by Quincy's moral vision as manifested in the politics of the Adams family, and particularly of Charles Francis Adams. The bargain struck between the Free Soil machine and the Massachusetts Democrats, making Sumner a senator and

Boutwell governor of the state, heralds the approaching failure of this artificial balance and an impending realignment of forces. The very train which takes the boy south is the harbinger of Southern defeat and Quincy's demise, a thought which concludes the chapter: "If ever in history men had been able to calculate on a certainty for a lifetime in advance, the citizens of the great Eastern seaports could do it in 1850 when their railway systems were already laid out" (3, p. 52). The mechanical age, symbolized by the railroad, has its center in Boston, not Washington or Quincy. If the railroad triumphs, then the agrarian South is defeated. And if the sectional equilibrium is destroyed, so also is Quincy, its source. The chapter thus concludes with the implied defeat of both the South and Quincy, and prepares logically for "Harvard College," where that defeat is prefigured in still another way.

Adams's denunciation of Harvard as a negative force has provoked defense of the school;[10] but severe as the charge may be—"Four years of Harvard College, if successful, resulted in an autobiographical blank" (4, p. 54)—the reader must remember that it logically proceeds from a man whose loyalties are with Quincy. From Adams's point of view, Harvard destroyed the dichotomies of Quincy's universe with a naïve transcendentalism which was tantamount to an adoption of Boston's truncated vision: "He was slipping away from fixed principles . . . ; from Quincy; and his first steps led toward Concord" (4, p. 63). A weakening of political interests accompanies this movement toward Concord —a serious undermining of Quincy's position, since, with the disappearance of the religious instinct, political action alone could effectively express the moral vision of life. Ironically, Harvard strengthens Adams's literary powers but leaves him without a message—form with no content! His personal situation clearly justifies the epithet "negative."

[10] See Samuels, *The Young Henry Adams,* pp. 8–52.

But negative forces have value, the reader learns, and "Harvard College" possesses a subtler value for the movement of the narrative by carrying the conflict of force in American life, heretofore described regionally, to its highest level of abstraction. The implied meanings of Boston and Washington as intellect and emotion become pinpointed in the persons of Adams and Rooney Lee, who act as specific incarnations of these energies. Adams "saw the New England type measure itself with another, and he was part of the process." "Strictly, the Southerner had no mind; he had temperament" (4, p. 57), and his total failure to integrate within the college community portends the destruction of the South in the coming holocaust.

The descriptions of the college body as a whole reflect the "scientific" bias of the chapter even more clearly. Harvard College is a negative force not only in its effect on the persona Adams but, within Adams's historical theory, as a symbol of thought itself. For Adams, thought is a single historical substance, a force with dissolvent properties which, because of its absorptive powers, can justly be called negative when one's self is the force being absorbed. In the "Rule of Phase" this characterization emerged through the metaphor of water:

This solvent, then, —this ultimate motion which absorbs all other forms of motion is an ultimate equilibrium, —this ethereal current of Thought, —is conceived as existing, like ice on a mountain range, and trickling from every pore of rock, in innumerable rills, uniting always into larger channels, and always dissolving whatever it meets, until at last it reaches equilibrium in the ocean of ultimate solution.[11]

In chapter 33 of the *Education,* too, the conception of thought as an agent assimilating all outside forces (p. 487) harmonizes with this later description of its dissolvent potential.

[11] *Degradation,* p. 281.

The picture of the Harvard milieu depends upon these notions; the young men possess the properties of a solution dissolving all forces and energies coming their way, and the first force to be absorbed is the Southerner: "Into this unusually dissolvent medium, chance insisted on enlarging Henry Adams's education by tossing a trio of Virginians" (4, p. 56). The students bear the mark of diverse molecules hanging loosely in solution: "Of unity this band of nearly one hundred young men had no keen sense, but they had equally little energy of repulsion" (4, p. 56). They exist only as latent energy: "What he could never measure was the bewildering impersonality of the men, who, at twenty years old, seemed to set no value either on official or personal standards" (4, p. 67). Finally, the determinism of the movement of thought, symbolized by this community, also appears through the metaphor of science:

They were objectiveness itself; their attitude was a law of nature; their judgment beyond appeal, not an act either of intellect or emotion or of will, but a sort of gravitation (4, p. 56).

As inevitably as the operations of a natural law, this "typical collection of young New Englanders" (4, p. 56), representative of the movement of thought, must triumph over Quincy and the South both. Underlying the random observations and personal rancor of "Harvard College," therefore, is a "scientific" structure depicting in quasi-chemical terms a critical moment in which two contradictory forces held in equilibrium are about to split apart.

Having scanned the forces in the unstable equilibrium of American life, Adams next journeys abroad, finally arriving at the chaos of Rome, the center of Western civilization. "Education went backward" (5, p. 73). Abroad, the same fracturing of forces in a highly unstable equilibrium which characterizes the American scene emerges to structure the narration of the young man's European education. The chapter on Berlin (5) opens with a series of tableaux evoking contradictory values and sweeping Adams panoramically into the past, from the nineteenth-century grime of the Black District with its Marxist overtones through eighteenth-century London back to Antwerp with its Renaissance painting and medieval cathedral. That the earlier phases of history clearly are residual, hanging in suspension for a moment before their destruction is complete, the narration never allows the reader to forget. "As a taste or a smell, it was education, especially because it lasted barely ten years longer" (5, p. 74). Berlin itself is medieval in educational method, with "the lecture system in its deadliest form as it flourished in the thirteenth century" (5, p. 75). Even this is temporary; the imagery of enclosure guiding the narrative implies an impending explosion which will vaporize these remnants of the past. German life was contained in foul rooms:

In all Berlin not a cubic inch of oxygen was admitted in winter into an inhabited building; in the school every room was tightly closed and had no ventilation; the air was foul beyond all decency; but when the American opened a window in the five minutes between hours, he violated the rules and was invariably rebuked. [5, p. 79]

As with learning, so with pleasure—pursued in smoky beer halls. A nation of prisoners, essentially disunited and held together artificially through the tyranny of state power, the Germans bore no resemblance to the metaphysical abstractions of Kant and Hegel who, positing unity, failed to account for the impending changes overtaking their own people.

The same angle of vision molds the experience of Adams in Rome. Medieval Rome may have been alive (6, p. 90), but this ancient energy exists within a framework of the Austro-Sardinian war and the famous expedition of Garibaldi resulting in the conquest of Sicily and Naples. The chapter on Rome is as carefully structured as that on Berlin—the medievalism of Rome hanging tenuously suspended in the web of revolutionary Italian change; the antiquity of Berlin, a remnant of the historic past symbolized by the opening tableaux, existing within the framework of the shuddering laughter of Heine and the insurrection of 1848. With Germany as with Italy, Adams telescopes time to see the eighteenth century as a single unit, extending from the medieval era: "The Germany he loved was the eighteenth century which the Germans were ashamed of" (6, p. 83), he observes in one breath; and in the next he allies that eighteenth century with the medieval past: "She was medieval by nature and geography, and this is what Adams, under the teachings of Carlyle and Lowell, liked" (6, p. 83). Similarly, ancient and medieval Rome merge in the present in Browning's stumbling across a guillotine fresh with the blood of a recent execution: "Adams . . . listened . . . to learn what new form of grim horror had for the moment wiped out the memory of two thousand years of Roman bloodshed" (6, p. 92). In both cases a vast continuum of time exists as a residuum within the framework of modern forces.

The technique is the same used to define the values of Quincy, which, like those cosmopolitan centers of culture, stands on the same brink of historical change. By duplicating the technique, Adams as artist extends in space the drama of the ending of a phase in history; hence the chapter on Rome fittingly climaxes all the young man's prior experience. Obsessed by the concept of the two falls of Rome, ancient and medieval, he unwittingly faces the most conclusive fall to date as the religious era in toto approaches extinction. Hence the chapter "Treason" (7) logically follows "Rome" and imparts a special meaning to his European venture. Here the narrative has ordered his European experience into polarities—forces of past and present—paralleling the polarities of South and North on the American continent. If opposing forces cannot coexist

in America, then by implication neither can the bipolar
European world remain intact. The structure of the narrative of Adams's London experience, in the chapters that
follow after a brief interlude in Washington, confirms this
inference by rendering specific European equivalents to the
forces in conflict in the new world.

Equivalences and Correspondences: The Creation of a Network of Force (Chapters 8–15)

The young Adams's English experience repeats the pattern
of his earlier life. Just as Quincy served as center for his
experiences in childhood and early youth, so here Yorkshire becomes a second Quincy possessing the same values
and magically, even fatefully, drawing Adams to itself. In
the complex of chapters from "Diplomacy" (8) through
"Darwinism" (15), the attraction gradually increases in intensity and provides a frame in which all other events are
ordered and measured. Fryston, the Yorkshire country seat
of Monckton Milnes, is the first line of Yorkshire force
compelling Adams, and "the singular luck that took him
to Fryston to meet the shock of the Trent Affair under
the sympathetic eyes of Monckton Milnes and William E.
Forster never afterwards deserted him" (8, p. 123). From
both these men Minister Adams draws strength in his pre-
carious early London days, and for both the minister and
his son it is the qualities of Yorkshire, microcosmically
represented in these its native sons, which sustain them.
"It was chiefly as education that this first country visit [to
Fryston] had value" (9, p. 138), Adams writes as his persona prepares for the country party which will introduce
him to Swinburne. He puzzles over Lothrop Motley's contention "that the London dinner and the English country
house were the perfection of human society" (8, p. 200),
for neither the food nor the conversation which he encountered justified the conclusion—save at Yorkshire:

Intimates are predestined. Adams met in England a thousand people, great and small; jostled against every one, from royal princes to gin-shop loafers; attended endless official functions and private parties; visited every part of the United Kingdom and was not quite a stranger at the Legations in Paris and Rome; he knew the societies of certain country houses, and acquired habits of Sunday-afternoon calls; but all this gave him nothing to do and was life wasted. . . . On the other hand, his few personal intimacies concerned him alone, and the chance that made him almost a Yorkshireman was one that must have started under the Heptarchy. [13, p. 205]

Adams stresses at great length the importance of Yorkshire because here he met Charles Milnes Gaskell, Francis Turner Palgrave, and a host of their friends with whom he retained a lifelong intimacy; but the emphasis which he gives to place is no mere eulogy proceeding from affectionate relationships. As a place, Yorkshire smacks of Quincy, and one must recall the relationship of Quincy to Boston to perceive the parallelism. "As a child of Quincy he was not a true Bostonian" (1, p. 19), the opening pages of the *Education* announce. What Adams calls "the inherited feud between Quincy and State Street" (2, p. 24) set the family apart from Boston:

For two hundred years, every Adams, from father to son, had lived within sight of State Street, and sometimes had lived in it, yet none had ever taken kindly to the town, or been taken kindly by it. [1, p. 9]

As for the boy, even in childhood "never for a moment did he connect the two ideas of Boston and John Adams . . . ; the idea of John Adams went with Quincy" (1, p. 10). Quincy was an influence that warped the mind, and its configurations led Adams naturally to Yorkshire:

More than any other county in England, Yorkshire retained a sort of social independence of London. Scotland itself was hardly more distinct. . . . London could never quite absorb Yorkshire, which, in its turn had no great love for London and freely showed it. To a certain degree, evident enough to Yorkshiremen, Yorkshire was not English—or was all England, as they might choose to express it. This must have been the reason why young Adams was drawn there rather than elsewhere. [13, pp. 205–6]

Within the immediate context, Adams's liking for Yorkshire at first appears to have no special meaning; he hates English society, and any departure from it can only be a welcome change. But within the larger framework of the book his Yorkshire preference emerges as a predetermined inclination molded through childhood experience, and hence the fatality with which Adams paints these Yorkshire events takes on a greater significance. Through this system of analogous reference, Adams as artist solves the problem of transforming his persona from a flesh-and-blood creature into a free-floating energy, possessed not of free will but of a magnetic capacity for following lines of force. Still very much an eighteenth-century man, his own force can be activated into meaningful shape and form only at Yorkshire because, as a channel of force and as a complex of values, it is equivalent to Quincy, an equivalence symbolically established through careful attention to place. As Quincy is to Boston, so Yorkshire is to London. And just as Adams can never be effective within the Boston milieu, so he is ineffectual in London; all of his meaningful experiences, culminating in the scene at Wenlock Abbey, occur either in Yorkshire or through the agency of Yorkshiremen.

This method is extended beyond relationships in place to include parallelisms in character types. Although Henry immediately doubts that his father can remain long in London—particularly as the young man not only foresees but even favors immediate war with England (8, p. 119)—sympathetic allies, a minority of the British to be sure, hail the minister and give him quick support. As types they reproduce the same pattern of personality possessed by Palfrey, Dana, and Sumner—supporters of the Free Soil party earlier founded by the minister. Like these New Englanders, Monckton Milnes and William E. Forster, both Yorkshire-men, possess a kind of balance between facade and interior reality. Only fools laughed at Milnes for his eccentricity, for this mere affectation concealed a steadiness of purpose and straightforward power which swept aside the genuine eccentricity of London society and gave him a broad influence corresponding to his extraordinary vitality (8, p. 124). Although Forster presented to the world a rough and un-gainly appearance, his facade concealed an "honest, unself-ish, practical" nature which led him to the Union cause "partly because of his Quaker anti-slavery convictions, and partly because it gave him a practical opening in the House. As a new member, he needed a field" (p. 125).

This contrast between inner resources and outward weak-ness recalls the poise which characterized Adams's father in chapter 2 and incarnates Milnes and Forster as types of the father, thus contributing to the values of Yorkshire as a second Quincy. Balance, too, describes both Cobden and Bright, who, although not from Yorkshire, are treated as a pair of the same type. The private secretary stands amazed before Bright's rough handling of English audi-ences. The man who could say, "We English are a nation of brutes, and ought to be exterminated to the last man" (12, p. 191) certainly appeared eccentric to an American mind; yet Adams's conclusion is different:

In all this, an American saw, if one may make the distinction, much racial eccentricity, but little that was personal. Bright was singularly well poised; but he used singularly strong language. [12, p. 190]

A certain irony develops throughout this section of the *Education* precisely because all the minister's allies are men of his own type and because Yorkshire, as a second Quincy, is the symbolic seat of his support. These same qualities, epitomized in the motif of *balance* and typified by Quincy, had failed to accomplish in America the same mission for which Minister Adams was sent to England. If he could not hold the forces of North and South in stable equilibrium in the States, as he had attempted to do when secession loomed on the horizon ("Treason" [7, p. 107]), how with the same resources could he effect the neutrality of England when only a minority of its people sympathized with the Union cause? In view of the minister's past record, Henry Adams's pessimism recurring throughout this period not only intensifies the irony of his father's position but strengthens the reader's doubts. "He modestly thought himself unfit for the career of adventurer, and judged his father to be less fit than himself" (8, p. 113), Adams says early in his London venture. And his characterization of their situation as "a family of early Christian martyrs about to be flung into an arena of lions, under the glad eyes of Tiberius Palmerston" (8, p. 114) is hardly overstatement. The private secretary judges their stay will be short:

He was mistaken—of course! He had been mistaken at every point of his education, and, on this point, he kept up the same mistake for nearly seven years longer, always deluded by the notion that the end was near. [8, p. 120]

This theme of the failure of Adams's education—a failure derived from his incorrect predictions all through his experience—is vital to an understanding of Adams's artistic intention here. The fact remains that all the young man's surmises are plausible: his father's inability to handle the situation, their impending departure from England, the deliberate malice of Russell, Palmerston, and Gladstone. Yet events do not bear any of them out. This is the heart of the matter. Just as there is a fatality in Adams's attraction to Yorkshire, so a fatality attends the entire struggle, diplomatic and military. Not till Adams as persona perceives that deterministic forces operate independent of human agency will he have education; but the careful reader need not remain ignorant of these forces, for the ignorance of Henry Adams is dramatized against a background of larger, impersonal energies shaping the seemingly chaotic experience of these pages.

On the level of pure diplomacy the two chapters "Political Morality" (10) and "The Battle of the Rams" (11) reveal one aspect of the impersonal operation of force as the decisive factor in the struggle. Here a reference to an earlier essay of Adams's, "The Declaration of Paris, 1861," is instructive because it analyzes the same material with a significant change in focus.[12] The essay evaluates the actions of Russell, as well as of his own father, in terms of national self-interest. The English seek the dissolution of a potentially dangerous power; Minister Adams behaves most untruculantly in the face of these provocations because of the special vulnerability of his strife-torn country, which could not afford to bring England openly into the war. But the angle of vision in the *Education* is radically different, deliberately obscuring reference to British national interests.

Repeatedly Adams emphasizes a distinction between history (which would interpret events as the essay does) and education. "As a part of Henry Adams's education it had a value distinct from history" (9, p. 136). He insists that "this was history, and had nothing to do with education" (11, p. 172). The focus of the chapters is the persona Adams's attempt to explain events according to the intentions of Russell and Palmerston, whom he perceives as hostile. What he encounters is "the sheer chaos of human nature" (10, p. 153) as these presumably trustworthy men continually deny the self-evident implications of their policies. The narrative thus creates a kaleidoscopic effect by measuring the successive conclusions of the persona against later evidence regarding British intentions, in order to create a chain of contradictory impressions and analyses of events for the

[12] In *Historical Essays,* (New York, 1891), pp. 237–78.

purpose of showing that neither Minister Adams nor, more importantly, the British diplomats are in control at any given moment. Apprentice Adams errs in crediting the Machiavellian Russell, Gladstone, and Palmerston with more power than they actually possess.

The final picture of Russell, not arrived at till much later, is mock-heroic: "Lord Russell had sacrificed the Lairds: had cost his Ministry the price of two ironclads, besides the Alabama Claims—say in round numbers twenty million dollars—and had put himself in the position of appearing to yield only to a threat of war" (11, p. 178). This final realization "upset from top to bottom the results of the private secretary's diplomatic education forty years after he had supposed it complete" (11, p. 178). Adams never tells the reader, but the reason for this upset is unmistakable. He realizes the impotence of the British statesmen as he had never done before. Ultimately they are no more in control than his father.

The immediate controls, of course, are the military forces represented by North and South raging in war on the American continent. The two chapters dealing with diplomatic warfare are hinged precisely on this struggle. On the defensive in "Political Morality," Minister Adams can take a more aggressive approach to the British in "The Battle of the Rams" (11)—even threaten war for their interference in American internal affairs (11, p. 172)—because of the turning point in the Civil War at the battles of Vicksburg and Gettysburg. The apprentice feels these forces:

Little by little, at first only as a shadowy chance of what might be, if things could be rightly done, one began to feel that, somewhere behind the chaos in Washington power was taking shape; that it was massed and guided as it had not been before . . . . the diplomatic campaign had to wait for the military campaign to lead. [11, p. 169]

The narrative explicitly states that force shapes and force

controls, and that individual human initiative is swallowed up in a larger, impersonal synthesis:

Politics cannot stop to study psychology . . . . All this knowledge would not have affected either the Minister or his son in 1862. The sum of the individuals would still have seemed, to the young man, one individual—a single will or intention—bent on breaking up the Union . . . . The individual would still have been identical with the mass. [10, p. 166]

The private secretary apprehends military force only, and if military power alone controls, the concept of force shaping human affairs remains on the human level and reduces itself to the triteness that might makes right. But there is a more complex vision of force operating here, consistent with Adams's historical theory, in which London society plays a major and, at first glance, confusing role. Recalling that Yorkshire and Quincy possess identical values, the reader easily enough equates London with Boston, an identification made all the more readily if one remembers an earlier chapter in which the tone of Boston life appears decidedly English (2, p. 28). In fact, the private secretary himself acted on this assumption, somewhat too hastily it would seem, as it occasioned one of the greatest shocks of life upon his official entrance into England at the beginning of the war:

He thought on May 12 that he was going to a friendly Government and people, true to the anti-slavery principles which had been their steadiest profession. For a hundred years the chief effort of his family had aimed at bringing the Government of England into intelligent cooperation with the objects and interests of America . . . . The slave States had been the chief apparent obstacle to good understanding. As for the private secretary himself, he was, like all Bostonians, instinctively English. He could not conceive the idea of a hostile England. [8, p. 114]

Instead of a world congenial to a Bostonian, however, Adams encounters an eccentric society, as he calls it, with distinctly southern values. To the English mind, Lincoln

and Seward were brute and demon; Thackeray wept and
Carlyle jibed (9, pp. 130–31). But the identification goes
further than sympathies. In "Eccentricity" (12) the whole
gamut of English society—its social, political, and intellectual representatives—is merged with representative southern types, and they are all of the same eccentric cast. Mason
and Slidell become indistinguishable from Lord Shaftesbury,
Fowell Buxton, and Gladstone. In fact this appears to be
the reason for Mason's failure as a Confederate representative: "In London society he counted merely as one eccentric
more" (12, p. 185). Here eccentricity is an imbalance origi-
nating in the preponderance of emotion over intellect; and
the English "threw their sympathies on the side which they
should naturally have opposed, and did so for no reason
except their eccentricity" (12, p. 184). Through this equation of England and the American South, the narrative tran-
scends the conception of force as military only, and extends
the conflict on American soil into a vaster drama of con-
flicting historical force. The portrayal of English society as
a whole is a vital part of this process, for in its looseness of
fabric it foreshadows the destruction of the South, its American equivalent.

The concept guiding this portrayal is the same which
underlay the earlier picture of the dissolution of New England federalism, and it will be well to repeat it here to
show the close correlation between conception and artistic
rendering. In the "Letter" Adams approved of this description of a nation's final deterioration:

"That which formed a people, a unity, a block, ends by becoming
an agglomeration of individuals without cohesion, still held together for a time by its traditions and institutions."[13]

"The Perfection of Human Society" characterizes English
life accordingly: "Society had no unity; one wandered about
in it like a maggot in cheese" (13, p. 197), a conception

[13] *Degradation,* p. 252.

supported artistically in the tableaux, presented successively, of Mme de Castiglione at Devonshire House and Garibaldi at Stafford House. Tableaux they are, and deliberately so. The aristocratic lady adored by a gaping mob of English aristocrats; Garibaldi worshiped by three duchesses, a scene ironically compared to Paolo Veronese's pictures of Christ's miracles. These tableaux stand next to each other and require relation of some kind, but the sequence between the two cannot yet be perceived by the persona.

The tableau technique reinforces the theme of social splintering and pointedly evokes the terms by which Adams later will solve his major problem, the failure of sequence in human affairs. Already art is connected with life, for these are living pictures. The problem of sequence requires the perception of force in pictures seemingly dead, and in "Dilettantism" (14) that problem assumes comic proportions as the experts display their inability to identify a Raphael save by the uncertain method of watermarks. The chapter is important: for through art as an embodier of historical force, Adams will later achieve an understanding of the evolution of historical force connecting past and present and explaining the disparate experiences in England as the demise of a religious era on a worldwide scale—an era whose symbol is art itself.

But there is another important observation to be made in connection with this portrayal of English life. If London and the South represent the same force—the one quietly dissolved, the other violently destroyed—then the reader seemingly can anticipate, through the terms of the correspondence already established, that if in England the Yorkshire point of view (sympathetic to the Union) will be victorious, then by implication Quincy (its American equivalent) will be victorious in America. Hence in "Darwinism" (15), although Adams instinctively shies away from a law of progress asserting evolution from lower to higher with its corollary of infinite improvement, he decides to act on Quincy precepts in his projected role as reformer. So he turns to the question of specie payments with a distinctly eighteenth-century bias controlling his thought: "His principles assured him that the honest way to resume payments was to restrict currency" (15, p. 233). His role as reformer is the active expression of social Darwinism, and Darwinism in turn is merely the reassertion of the values of Quincy in another form: "The Church was gone, and Duty was dim, but Will should take its place" (15, p. 232). Thus Adams turns to America hopefully, and the system of equations operating throughout suggests that this hope might be well founded. Although the reader knows that State Street awaits Adams with renewed vigor, the persona Henry Adams could not yet predict the future: "No one could yet guess which of his contemporaries was most likely to play a part in the great world" (15, p. 234).

Read in the light of this system of equations and the dialectic of Adams's historical theory, this complex of chapters (8–15) takes on an order quite as deliberate as that of the opening ones. In the first group Adams moves through a series of power centers—from Quincy, the last stronghold of the eighteenth century and the religious phase; to Boston, the heart of New England and representative of a mechanical phase; through Washington, center of the nation and heart of the slavocracy; to Berlin and Rome, fathers of metaphysical unity and Western civilization respectively.[14] After the transitional chapter "Treason," which destroys the tentative equilibrium of forces depicted in the first complex of chapters, the second group studies the breakdown in a more concentrated form. The chapters from "Diplomacy" through "The Perfection of Human Society" (8–13) form a single unit, in the first half of which individual character types symbolize a realignment of the same forces contending in America (8–10) and, in the second half, where

[14] Lyon (chapter 6) has also made identification of place calling each a capital: for example, Quincy, of the eighteenth century; Berlin, of metaphysics; Rome, of Western civilization.

the equilibrium of force breaks in favor of Yorkshire, the equivalent of the Southern force (London society itself) dissolves to parallel the destruction of the South. Chapters 14 and 15, "Dilettantism" and "Darwinism," display the effects of the English experience on Adams; here he wavers between the dilettantism of a fractured universe and the more respectable ideal of unity for which he has long striven. But Darwinism as faith runs contrary to a degradationist scheme of history, and in the third complex of chapters, that degradationist bias emerges to create a powerful scheme of ironies.

Physical Force and Social Events: The Narrative Pattern (Chapters 16–20)

The complex of chapters from "The Press" (16) through "Failure" (20) possesses two distinct but related movements giving the section a special unity of its own while simultaneously connecting it with the broader artistic process of the *Education*. The first level of movement[15] is thematic and dramatizes the ironic disparity between Adams's Darwinian evangelism, realized in action by his efforts at reform through political writing, and its dismal failure. The climax of this movement is "Failure" (20), wherein Adams withdraws triply by abandoning reform, politics, and Washington itself for a career as history teacher at Harvard. The center of this movement is political, revolving about President Grant's ineptitude as administrator and leader—an incompetence which both fired Adams's zeal by providing scandals aplenty for him to attack and finally destroyed that zeal through the magnitude of the ineptness: "Not one young man of promise remained in the Government service.

[15] Levenson has observed in this section the double references of the chapter titles—relating both to nature and to man in "Free Fight" and "Chaos." He thinks of "Free Fight" as having Darwinian overtones. He notices a juxtaposition of nature's chaos and social chaos but does not connect this with a structure dependent upon a deterministic view of history (pp. 319–21).

All drifted into opposition . . . . Adams's case was perhaps
the strongest because he thought he had done well" (19, p.
296). Hence, the abrupt removal to Harvard:

So, at twenty-four hours' notice, he broke his life in halves again
in order to begin a new education, on lines he had not chosen, in
subjects for which he cared less than nothing; in a place he did
not love, and before a future which repelled. [19, p. 294]

The pronouncement that life was severed in two has relevance not only to the failure of his Washington career but
also to the demise of a viable motive force in history. The
failure of Darwinism proceeds from the young man's Washington experience and from the events in "Chaos," with its
climactic portrayal of his sister's death. "The progress of
evolution from President Washington to President Grant,
was alone evidence enough to upset Darwin" (17, p. 266),
he observes—an observation leading him not to a theory
of reversion, which "was more absurd than that of evolution" (p. 266), but to a sense of political chaos imaged in
the scandals provoked by Gould and Fisk and the wild in-
fighting between Sumner and Fish, Chase and Hoar, which
threatens the very fabric of constitutional government.

The scene of his sister's death goes beyond the social
vision of national chaos to a perception of anarchic forces
operating behind the stage scenery of nature: "For the first
time in his life, Mont Blanc for a moment looked to him
what it was—a chaos of anarchic and purposeless forces"
(19, p. 289). But the momentary vision of natural chaos
merges once again with the human scene, this time inter-
nationalized by the outbreak of the Franco-Prussian War.
Adams is left with a sense of purposelessness in nature and
man totally contravening the postulates of Darwinism, with
its conception of infinite progress. Thus the "Failure" by
which he characterizes his academic career becomes not the
pose of disillusionment adopted by a belated romantic, but
the bitter irony of one forced to teach history according to
logical sequences shortly after experience has shown him

that chaos is the law of nature and of men. The thematic movement thus logically leads to the academic dilemma of "Failure." "Adams found himself obliged to force his material into some shape to which a method could be applied" (20, pp. 302–3), but this violates truth. "In essence incoherent and immoral, history had either to be taught as such—or falsified" (20, p. 301).

Although Adams as persona sees only anarchy, the matured Adams as artist shapes the narrative structure of these chapters to show that human energy is diminished in a mechanical phase of history where extrahuman forces seek their own equilibrium independent of human control. This is the second level of movement within the chapters. A process which began early in the narrative finally comes into its own in "The Press" (16), in which the consolidating energies of a rising industrial capitalism symbolize the victory of Boston values in the new America. In a chapter that concludes the book, Adams writes:

> Images are not arguments, rarely even lead to proof, but the mind craves them . . . . The image needed here is that of a new centre, or preponderating mass, artificially introduced on earth in the midst of a system of attractive forces that previously made their own equilibrium, and constantly induced to accelerate its motion till it shall establish a new equilibrium. A dynamic theory would begin by assuming that all history, terrestrial or cosmic, mechanical or intellectual, would be reducible to this formula if we knew the facts. [34, p. 489]

This conception guides the narrative movement of "The Press," in which the railroad reemerges[16] as the symbol of

[16] The image of the railroad is important in chapters 1 (pp. 5, 22) and 3 (pp. 43, 52). Mentioned in passing in chapter 6 (p. 83), it does not really assume importance again till the reference in "Darwinism" (15, p. 229), where it becomes related by inference to a mechanical phase of history—as earlier—and then takes on significance in the following chapters as a sign of the approaching climax of the mechanical era. The climax is reached in "Chicago" (22, p. 344) with the adoption of the gold standard—an economic climax foreshadowed by the growth of the railway system in "Twenty Years After" (21, p. 330).

mechanical energy drawing all human movement to itself. "The generation between 1865 and 1895 was already mortgaged to the railways" (16, p. 240). "Boston meant business. The Bostonians were building railways" (p. 241). Returning to Washington by train, Adams surveys an eighteenth-century society existing as a crumbling facade above the newly emergent center of force replacing the State Department: the Treasury (16, p. 247)—the natural corollary of the railroads and of State Street. And man remains passive before these terrifying economic forces.

This loss of human energy in American life consequent upon its passage into a new phase appears in the weakening of intellect, represented most graphically by Grant. In this chapter ("President Grant" 17), the president's failure to act constructively on his platform announcements of reform is linked specifically to deficiencies of thought. The reaction which Adams as reformer displays toward Grant at once suggests his rejection of social Darwinism and bitingly satirizes the president by his observation that Grant represents evolution in reverse. Yet "Grant's administration reverted to nothing. One could not catch a trait of the past, still less of the future. It was not even sensibly American" (17, p. 266). Thus the narrative emphasizes the decline of human energies, since the administration has so succumbed to mechanical force that it defies the appellation "American"; and this decline is perfectly imaged in the career of Grant himself, who moved from the leadership of battle, where he had displayed his ability to act purposively, to the leadership of the nation in peace, where he failed to act at all. To Adams, "Grant appeared as an intermittent energy, immensely powerful when awake, but passive and plastic in repose" (17, p. 264); and this lack of human control in the new order appears most distinctly in "Free Fight" (18).

Jay Gould's Gold Conspiracy and James Fisk's questionable manipulation of Erie stock, in partnership with Gould, certainly suggest that the troubles in post–Civil War American life are man-made; and the essays on these scandals which Henry and his brother Charles Francis, Jr., wrote at the time have as their object the pinpointing of personal responsibility on the figures involved.[17] But in the *Education* the scandals take on somewhat altered values, existing to show the operation of blind force which contaminates the republic and in whose centralizing power the nation acquiesces. Repeatedly Adams stresses the universality of corruption:

The worst scandals of the eighteenth century were relatively harmless by the side of this, which smirched executive, judiciary, banks, corporate systems, professions, and people, all the great active forces of society, in one dirty cesspool of vulgar corruption. [18, pp. 271–72]

But Gould and Fisk are part of the railway system, and the same forces which corrupt also draw the nation's energies to themselves into a unity:

They [Americans] had to content themselves by turning their backs and going to work harder than ever on their railroads and foundries. They were strong enough to carry even their politics. [18, p. 273]

Clearly there is a pattern in this chaos, and what Adams as persona sees as "the game of cross-purposes" (18, p. 278) provides an important clue to the underlying method. He puzzles over the fate and behavior of two important men:

That Sumner and Hoar, the two New Englanders in great position who happened to be the two persons most necessary for his success at Washington, should be the first victims of Grant's lax rule, must have had some meaning for Adams's education, if Adams could only have understood what it was. . . . His four most powerful friends had matched themselves, two and two, and

[17] In Henry Adams and Charles F. Adams, Jr., *Chapters of Erie* (Boston, 1871): Henry Adams, "The New York Gold Conspiracy," pp. 100–134; Charles Francis Adams, Jr., "A Chapter of Erie," pp. 1–99.

were fighting in pairs to a finish; Sumner-Fish; Chase-Hoar; with foreign affairs and the judiciary as prizes! What value had the fight in education? [18, p. 279]

The literal historical issues here are quite complicated, but certain facts seem sure and give significance to the narrative pattern. Sumner opposed the annexation of the Dominican Republic, thus incurring the wrath of Grant. Secretary of State Fish, probably reluctantly, went along with Grant and incurred the wrath of Sumner. As Adams presents the case, Sumner was responsible for the rupture with Fish; and he makes the focal issue Sumner's demand for the cession of Canada to the United States as compensation for English interference in the Civil War (18, p. 275). Significantly, the Grant Administration, described as a vacuum, is ultimately responsible for the free fight of these pages. "Between these great forces [Sumner vs. Fish and Grant], where was the Administration and how was one to support it? One must first find it, and even then it was not easily caught" (18, p. 276).

In the fight between Supreme Court Justice Chase and Attorney General Hoar, the issue was even more clouded. Adams respected Hoar for his persistent and courageous fight against the spoils system. He also liked the court's overturning, by just one vote and with the concurrence of Chase, the constitutionality of the Legal Tender Act of 1862—at least that portion of the act which made greenbacks legal tender at the time it was passed. When the act was repealed, Grant appointed two new members to the court, opening himself to charges that he was stacking the judiciary to get his own way. (Grant wanted the constitutionality of the act upheld.) Ironically, Chase as former secretary of the treasury under Lincoln had been responsible for its issuance. Just as ironic for Adams, the attorney general whom he respected led an attack on Chase's reversed decision—an attack which made Adams sympathize with the justice for reasons other than a natural repugnance for paper money.[18] The very sanctity of the court was threatened. "He still clung to the Supreme Court, much as a churchman clings to his bishops, because they are his only symbol of unity; his last rag of Right" (18, p. 277). But whether the issue was a dissolution of the Administration, which Adams initially had hoped to support, or the Administration's threat to the moral authority of the court, delivered by a man with whom Adams sympathized, the pattern established here is consistent with Adams's vision of the historical process. "A society in stable equilibrium is—by definition—one that has no history and wants no historians," he later observed.[19] Although American society persists, in "Free Fight" he portrays the final death of its older concepts through the neutralizing equilibrium which its old guard brings about. The meaning is clear. Human power has dwindled.

Just as *balance* appears as a key word in the earlier chapters of the *Education*, to suggest that human acts still possess some relevance in a universe where force is imaged mainly in social and political terms, so *drift* becomes a repeated verbal reference in these later chapters, to image the diminution of human force in the new mechanical phase of history.[20] At first lost in a world of office-seekers, Adams "drifted among them, unnoticed"; he "floated with the stream." "Grant avowed from the start a policy of drift; and a policy of drift attaches only barnacles" (17, pp. 255,

[18] A useful, brief background on the fight between Sumner and Fish can be found under the entry for Hamilton Fish, the *Dictionary of American Biography* (New York, 1931): 398–99. For Adams's attitude toward Sumner, see especially the Letter to Carl Schurz, 16 May 1871, Ford, 1: 208. On Adams's respect for Hoar, see Samuels, *The Young Henry Adams*, p. 190. On his attitude toward the Legal Tender Act of 1862, see the same volume, p. 155. On Adams's position with respect to the repeal of parts of this act, see the same volume, p. 192.

[19] "Letter," *Degradation*, p. 248.

[20] Other critics have noticed this emphasis upon drift. For example, Levenson (p. 323) associates it with death.

262, 267). "Henry Adams went on, drifting further and further from the Administration" (18, p. 278). "All drifted into opposition" (19, p. 296). In the person of Adams, this loss of will reaches a minor climax in his ineffective protests against going to Harvard. (Four full pages of the narrative [19, pp. 293–97] are devoted to explaining that he had nothing whatever to do with the move.) It reaches a major climax in the account of his meeting with King at Estes Park, in which the renewed theme of the predestined character of friendships, here dramatized against the vastness of space and time, culminates in the statement:

The one, coming from the west, saturated with the sunshine of the Sierras, met the other, drifting from the east, drenched in the fogs of London. [20, p. 312]

Later it will be seen that the emphasis upon the direction of Adams's movement evokes the concept of the *translatio studii,* and thus the meeting with King foreshadows the scientific synthesis of historical and personal experience which is the focus of the final section of the *Education.* "The lines of their lives converged, but King had moulded and directed his life logically, scientifically, as Adams thought American life should be directed" (20, p. 312). So the *drift* of these pages implies not only a loss of human energy but a movement toward a scientific resolution of man's experience in a universe directed by physical force; and the need for such a resolution is displayed by a narrative structure which implies a *necessary* connection between physical force and social events.

The structure of "Free Fight" (18) and "Chaos" (19) prepares for the meeting with King, which promises to transform failure into success. The former chapter possesses a framework concentrating on details of physical nature, opening with a picture of the beauties of a Washington spring—"sensual, animal, and elemental"—the very denial of any terrors lurking beneath nature's surface implying that they might be there, merely hidden from view:

Here and there a negro log cabin alone disturbed the dogwood and the judas-tree, the azalea and the laurel. The tulip and the chestnut gave no sense of struggle against a stingy nature. The soft, full outlines of the landscape carried no hidden horror of glaciers in its bosom. [18, p. 268]

Those concealed terrors merge with the theme of Grant's deception regarding his platform pronouncements—a theme immediately following the sensuous description of a deceptive nature: "In spite of the fatal deception—or undeception—about Grant's political character, Adams's first winter in Washington had amused him" (p. 268).

The implied terrors of nature become real in the political scene revolving about Grant's administration. The conspiracies of Gould and Fisk, together with the fights of Sumner and Hoar against Fish and Chase become related by inference to the concealed agencies of destruction in nature. The inference is made unmistakable in the chapter's conclusion where "the judas-tree," the symbol of betrayal and destruction, is conjoined with the political life of Washington in a paragraph establishing specific correspondence between nature and politics and between Washington and Rome:

When spring came, he took to the woods, which were best of all, for after the first of April, what Maurice de Guérin called "the vast maternity" of nature showed charms more voluptuous than the vast paternity of the United States Senate. Senators were less ornamental than the dogwood or even the judas-tree. They were, as a rule, less good company. Adams astonished himself by remarking what a purified charm was lent to the Capitol by the greatest possible distance, as one caught glimpses of the dome over miles of forest foliage. At such moments he pondered on the distant beauty of St. Peter's and the steps of Ara Coeli. [18, p. 282]

Thus nature, the apparent chaos of American political life, and, with the reference to Ara Coeli, the concept of historical phase are brought together. "Chaos" continues this pattern but with a significant reversal of emphasis. Whereas the details of nature create a framework within which political experience is couched in "Free Fight" (18), political experience creates the framework within which a vision of natural force is couched in "Chaos" (19).

The opening framework of the latter chapter consists of observations on the progress of reform in England, culminating in Reeve's refusal to print Adams's essay on the gold conspiracy, a refusal generated by fear of the power of Gould and Fisk (19, p. 286), who figure in the main body of chapter 18. The last part of the framework, the outbreak of the Franco-Prussian War and Adams's departure for Harvard, continues the theme of political chaos which was the focus of the earlier chapter. Within this framework the death of the sister is dramatically rendered all the more horrible through the skillful contrast between the sensuality of the Italian countryside at Bagni di Lucca and the violence of pain and suffering within the sickroom. The succeeding vision of Mont Blanc climaxes the theme of destructive natural force concealed within nature—a theme which was the subject of the framework of chapter 18, "Free Fight."

The total interpenetration of the two chapters (18 and 19)—the framework of the one existing as the focus of the other, and vice versa—apotheosizes a double vision of physical force and social events and renders a vital connection between the two. It must be remembered that the persona does not perceive this vital connection. In "Chaos" he apprehends the vision of Mont Blanc as a mere psychological projection of his sense of personal anarchy consequent upon his witnessing the death of his sister: "the fantastic mystery of coincidences had made the world, which he thought real, mimic and reproduce the distorted nightmare of his personal horror" (19, p. 289). For him the political events of "Free Fight" and the outbreak of the Franco-Prussian War bear no necessary relationship to the vision of anarchic force destroying his sister and wildly operating behind the beauties of Mont Blanc. It is the structure of the narrative which artistically creates the relationship. The meeting with King in "Failure" (20), then, is a denouement following this climax ("Chaos") and foreshadows, as observed earlier, a scientific understanding of the relation of natural physical force to human events.

The Paradoxical Vision (Chapters 21–35)

Following Adams's declarations of "Failure" in the chapter so named, the book's concluding chapters (21–35) seem a mere hodgepodge of illustrations of the idea of multiplicity. Levenson's view is representative:

He meant to have intellect take over as imagination began to falter so that his narrative would proceed past its second climax until it reached not the Thomist synthesis of scholastic science but a synthetic theory of history couched in a more modern scientific language. However, as he warned in his "Editor's Preface," "the scheme became unmanageable as he approached his end." Unfortunately, when the imagination faltered, the mind was tired. There were half a dozen ways to get to his conclusion, but Adams, brim full of things to say and hopeful that his intuition would organize all, tried one way after another. Each of them was interesting, but the series became an intricate confusion.[21]

But Adams's admission of a failure in form nonetheless entails a conception of some overriding form existing almost independent of the subject matter. To repeat his words to Edith Morton Eustis, "Our point of vision regards only the form—not the matter . . . . I can see where the form fails, but I cannot see how to correct the failures. I believe the scheme impossible."[22] The critic's job is to perceive the intended form, failure though it may be, and the task is not so impossible or hypothetical as it may at first appear, precisely because of Adams's commitment to the principle of organicism. Having observed the deliberateness of the structure within the first twenty chapters of the *Education,* the reader can, by using it as a measure, observe

[21] Levenson, p. 333.
[22] 28 [February 1908?], Cater, pp. 614–15.

its relationship to the last chapters and thus arrive at the basic conception intended to yield formal unity to the book's conclusion. In so doing, furthermore, the nature of Adams's failure will be considerably modified, becoming not so much a personal incapacity for rendering artistic unity as what he probably meant when he said, "I believe the scheme impossible"—his arrival at the limits of art itself.

Adams's basic problem throughout the first part of the book has been twofold: How can he relate the past to the present? And how can he integrate the warring faculties of emotion and intellect? The narrative, as the reader has seen, inextricably relates the historical to the personal; and in the second part, the mode by which Adams arrives at his theory of history solves the problem on both levels as he perceives the values of what he once called "education only sensual" and prepares for the grand synthesis of experience concluding the *Education*.

The preparation for this synthesis occurs within a framework heralding the triumph of the mechanical phase of history as the machinery of politics and the national economy centralizes about the new forces heretofore symbolized by the railroad. Paradoxically, the framework also forecasts the demise of this mechanical phase when it is at its zenith because the introduction of supersensual forces predicts yet a succeeding era in historical experience. The victory of "the capitalistic system with all its necessary machinery" (22, p. 344) is signaled by the adoption of the single gold standard— a victory seen as inevitably proceeding from the financial panic of 1893. But the panic was only the external form of a drama of blind force operating beyond the control of man:

Blindly some very powerful energy was at work, doing something that nobody wanted done. . . . Evidently the force was one; its operation was mechanical; its effect must be proportional to its power; but no one knew what it meant, and most people dismissed it as an emotion—a panic—that meant nothing. [22, p. 338]

The dynamos which Adams views at the Chicago Exposition introduce the theme, later elaborated, of supersensual forces which "gave to history a new phase" by rupturing "the unity of natural force" (22, p. 342). And public response to the St. Gaudens figure, embodying "the oldest idea known to human thought" (21, p. 329)—"the idea of Thought" itself—or contemplation,[23] symbolizes the degradation of human thought as it passes into a new phase:

None felt what would have been a nursery-instinct to a Hindu baby or a Japanese jinricksha-runner. The only exceptions were the clergy, who taught a lesson even deeper. One after another brought companions there, and, apparently fascinated by their own reflection, broke out passionately against the expression they felt in the figure of despair, of atheism, of denial. Like the others, the priest saw only what he brought. Like all great artists, St. Gaudens held up the mirror and no more. The American layman had lost sight of ideals; the American priest had lost sight of faith. [21, p. 329]

The break of twenty years in the book's time sequence, hence, is guided by the theory of phase, and it symbolizes through triple reference the consummation of the historical fracturing shown in process in the earlier sections. But the gap has relevance to the persona as well. In the meeting with King (see "Failure"), Adams's physical movement—a "drifting from the east, drenched in the fogs of London" (p. 312)—symbolizes the entire character of his education. The emphasis upon direction is important, evoking as it does the traditional concept that the movement of knowledge is from east to west, the same as the movement of empire. Adams's movement thus emphasizes the traditional nature of an education ironically at variance with the move-

[23] The meaning of the figure's expression has been defined in several ways, always implying total peace or the expression of the inevitable. Adams suggested it meant Thought in a letter to Elizabeth Cameron, 19 April 1903, Ford, 2: 407. See also Cater, cxviii; Stevenson, caption under picture opposite p. 222.

ment of history which, entering a new phase, rejects tradition. (King, as scientist, moved from west to east.) "Twenty Years After" renews this theme of physical movement to symbolize the final separation of Adams from a changed world—a separation heretofore occurring gradually but reaching its climax in the first two chapters of the concluding section. He was drenched in the fogs of London when he met King in Estes Park. Now the reader finds him in a London hospital bed. "He had just come up from the South Seas with John La Farge" (21, p. 316). Thus his drift from east to west has brought him to the South Seas and back to his starting point, where he must begin a new education, although reluctantly:

Adams would rather, as choice, have gone back to the east [the South Seas], if it were only to sleep forever in the trade-winds under the southern stars, wandering over the dark purple ocean, with its purple sense of solitude and void. Not that he liked the sensation, but that it was the most unearthly he had felt. He had not yet happened on Rudyard Kipling's "Mandalay," but he knew the poetry before he knew the poem, like millions of wanderers, who have perhaps alone felt the world exactly as it is. Nothing attracted him less than the idea of beginning a new education. The old one had been poor enough; any new one could only add to its faults. [21, pp. 316–17]

As earlier, this traditional education, one preparing him for the past rather than the future, again is associated with art, and through its symbolism the total alienation of Adams from the present emerges most clearly. Returning from "tropical islands, mountain solitudes, archaic law, and retrograde types" (23, p. 350), he renews the theme of "education only sensual" by observing that "infinitely more amusing and incomparably more picturesque than civilization, they educated only artists, and, as one's sixtieth year approached, the artist began to die" (pp. 350–51). Hence, he turns to the new world with statistics, "taking for granted that the alternative to art was arithmetic" (p. 351).

The first five chapters (21–25) repeatedly emphasize art as a symbol both of the alienation of the persona from his contemporary world and of historical change, beginning with the reference to the St. Gaudens figure (21, p. 329), continuing through references to Richard Hunt's architecture at the Chicago Exposition (22, p. 340), to the Normandy cathedrals and churrigueresque architecture of Mexico (23, pp. 354–55), to the meeting with La Farge and Whistler (24, pp. 369–71), and climaxing in "The Dynamo and the Virgin" (25). Other supports of the theme are the marked use of window imagery (21, pp. 326–27) to display Adams as a spectator at life's new feast and the repeated allusions to 'slack water" (p. 325) and "dead water of the *fin-de-siècle*" (22, p. 331; 23, p. 346). The dead water is the sole reminder of the past which will be swept away absolutely by the enveloping flood of new forces, coming to a climax in the destruction of all of Adams's class: "The whole mechanical consolidation of force . . . ruthlessly stamped out the life of the class into which Adams was born" (22, p. 345).

But this last catastrophe, curiously enough, stimulates Adams to renew his search for unity of experience: "The old machine ran far behind its duty; . . . it was bound to break down, and if it happened to break precisely over one's head, it gave the better chance for study" (22, p. 338). Thus the historical process creating Adams's sense of personal alienation paradoxically places him in the mainstream of historical movement. Associated with the theme of death (26, p. 396), the persona's movement to personal disintegration becomes the movement of history itself, so that Adams, "floundering through the corridors of chaos" (26, p. 402), for the first time no longer is at odds with the temporal continuum: "After so many years of effort to find one's drift, the drift found the seeker" (29, p. 426). This new sense of identification with the world points the way to a hitherto untried method of achieving unity of experience in which art plays a role the reverse of its function seen thus far.

To understand the unity of the first five chapters of this section, it is important to recognize that the dichotomies between the form of art and the shapeless present seen in each of them lead Adams to a conscious realization of the process heretofore only implicit in the book—that he himself is a microcosm of the historical continuum and therefore a valid center for understanding the whole of history. In "Twilight" (26), the sixth and pivotal chapter of the entire section, this awareness becomes explicit as Adams surveys the drift in history from a political level, on which Hay operates, and from a scientific level, on which King moves. History in both these spheres possesses the same movement from unity to multiplicity which he finds in his own life, and Adams specifically correlates the personal, the scientific, and the political in the anguished outburst:

The magnet in its new relation staggered his new education by its evidence of growing complexity, and multiplicity, and even contradiction, in life. He could not escape it; politics or science, the lesson was the same, and at every step it blocked his path whichever way he turned. He found it in politics; he ran against it in science; he struck it in everyday life, as though he were still Adam in the Garden of Eden between God who was unity, and Satan who was complexity, with no means of deciding which was truth. The problem was the same for McKinley as for Adam, and for the Senate as for Satan. Hay was going to wreck on it, like King and Adams. [26, pp. 397–98]

If this correlation of levels of experience is fair, Adams can operate from the inside out—and by giving unity to his own experience, provide unity within history as well. That this is his intention can be observed by references to the private nature of the attempted synthesis. Before launching into the final triad of chapters, containing the most generalized expression of the theory, he calls attention to its highly individual character:

One sought no absolute truth. One sought only a spool on which to wind the thread of history without breaking it. Among indefinite possible orbits, one sought the orbit which would best satisfy the observed movement of the runaway star Groombridge, 1838, commonly called Henry Adams. As term of a nineteenth-century education, one sought a common factor for certain definite historical fractions. Any schoolboy could work out the problem if he were given the right to state it in his own terms. [32, pp. 472–73]

Therefore, the organization of the last section has two basic parts connected by "Twilight" (26). In the first (21–25), the persona achieves a personal synthesis of experience which, in "Twilight" (26) he identifies with the movement of history. The rest of the narrative is a projection of the personal synthesis onto the outer world in an attempt to achieve a unified vision of history. In short, the experiment has come full circle. Using the self as a measure of relation Adams judged the past in the *Chartres*. Now he will consciously judge the present and the future.

Chapters 21–25 display Adams's gradual integration of sense with intellect to achieve a unity of those warring elements whose conflict formed a large part of the earlier narrative. The chance meeting with La Farge is central here because it replaces his naïve notion of "education only sensual" with an awareness of the cognitive processes of art. La Farge "had no difficulty in carrying different shades of contradiction in his mind" (24, p. 370) because he thought like an artist, valuing symbols for their resolution of apparent contradictions. "In conversation La Farge's mind was opaline with infinite shades and refractions of light, and with color toned down to the finest gradations" (p. 371), a method of thought quite opposed to that of the ordinary mind which likes to "walk straight up to its object, and assert or deny something that it takes for a fact" (p. 369). "The mind resorts to reason for want of training, and Adams had never met a perfectly trained mind" (p. 370).

Armed with this recognition of art as a way of knowing, Adams seeks to apply the method to history itself.

The first four chapters juxtapose the values of art against the shapeless present in a way demanding relationship. The process begins with showing the total separation from the ignorant public of the ideals incarnated in the St. Gaudens figure (21). It continues with the curious juxtaposition of Richard Hunt's classical architecture against the industrial exhibits of the Chicago Exposition (22), thus posing the question of historical continuity (p. 340); it is maintained in the contrast between art and arithmetic in "Silence" (23) and in that chapter's numerous dichotomies between art and society. The chapter's most important contrast is the shift from a legalistic German view of medieval history to the knowledge of art which gives Adams "a new sense of history" (pp. 354–55). All of these dichotomies, with art as one polar element, converge in "Indian Summer" to demand a symbolic interpretation of history. There Adams perceives that following a single strand of development—law, or religion, or politics—cannot explain the whole (p. 368). "Everything must be made to move together" (p. 378). To do this, only an expansive symbolism will suffice, for through symbol the artist can unify the multiplicity of experience; and thus the meeting with La Farge, where he apprehends the values of symbolic methods of thought, is an important preparation for the climax of the book.

"The Dynamo and the Virgin" (25) most explicitly brings together the two strands of previous experience, personal and historical, by emphasizing feeling and self. Just as Adams responds to the dynamo with a prayer (25, p. 380), so too men once prayed to the Virgin. By using the feeling self as center, he might be able to measure the respective force of each. Such an experiment might solve the historical problem of sequence in history, since these two forces represent different historical epochs. But it would also solve his personal problem of synthesizing his warring faculties of sense and intellect, since the basis of the experiment was to treat these symbols "as they had been felt; as convertible, interchangeable attractions on thought" (25, p. 383). To feel the force of the Virgin, he must approach her subjectively through her art, and in so doing he can satisfy his aesthetic nature. But to articulate those relationships between the symbols which he instinctively feels, he must bring the intellect into play. Even if he can recapture the force of the Virgin, Adams observes:

The historian's business was to follow the track of the energy; to find where it came from and where it went to; its complex source and shifting channels; its values, equivalents, conversions. [25, p. 389]

The values of the two symbols are founded in feeling which, acting as a base for the intellect, solves the problem of synthesizing the two faculties of the persona while simultaneously solving the historical problem of sequence as well. Deliberately maintaining the fiction that the *Chartres* was conceived with the *Education* in mind, he can thus assert that the terms of his "scientific" experiment are set. The result of the effort to find where the energy of the Virgin came from is Adams's earlier book, *Mont-Saint-Michel and Chartres*. The first part of the *Education* displays the breakdown of medieval unity according to a system of equivalences and correspondences, as has already been observed. After "Twilight," the narrative symbolically traces its equivalents and conversions on a larger scale.

Since by "Twilight" (26) Adams has recognized the possibility of using his own life to understand the process of history, he necessarily sees that the unity which he seeks in history can only be a projection of the self. Approaching the Bergsonian notion of *durée,* he finally pictures his persona as tentatively holding together both poles of history—unity and multiplicity—in an amusing concluding episode in which he uses the automobile to visit the sacred monu-

ments to the Virgin (32, p. 469). This is the logical conclusion
to the entire experiment conducted in the *Chartres* and the
Education. Since the experiment was postulated upon measuring force by the self, then as center of the historical movement from unity to chaos Adams logically seeks to project
upon all the world the paradoxical vision that unity and
chaos are one. His double view of medieval life in the *Chartres* apprehended the reality of complex force behind the
apparent unity of the medieval world. So too, in the final
chapters of the *Education*, the unities he perceives are visions
of chaos as well.

From "Teufelsdröckh" through "Vis Nova" (27–32) the
vision of the Conservative Christian Anarchist dominates
the narrative, and it is a double vision, perceiving simultaneously order and chaos prevailing in every area of experience. Before investigating the mode through which
Adams expresses this paradox, the critic must account for
its implementation. There are four reasons. First, in the role
of Conservative Christian Anarchist, Adams as persona
achieves his ultimate status as a microcosm of the historical
continuum moving from the unity of the Virgin, who draws
all activities toward her, to the diffraction of the dynamo,
which introduces so many new forces on the scene that his
mind, and by implication society's, lose a sense of unity. As
such the simultaneous vision of order and anarchy is perfectly appropriate to the terms of his original experiment.

Second, such a vision satisfies Adams's theory of history,
particularly as it is expressed in the "Rule of Phase." There
Adams draws the analogy between the modes of existence of
a physical substance and the relationship of phases in history. Just as ice, water, and vapor are three modes of the
familiar fluid water, so a religious, a mechanical, an electrical, and an ethereal phase of human history are all different modes (or phases) of the same substance, thought.
But just as water is more tangible than its gaseous phase,
vapor, so a religious phase possesses a more apparent unity

than, say, the mechanical phase, where a leveling of society in the transition from aristocratic hierarchies to democracies corresponds to the seeming anarchy of vapor. Unity becomes chaos, thus, according to this view of history, although the chaos possesses all the elements of an older order.

Third, this vision lends itself to the analogy of Hegel and Schopenhauer, from whom the Conservative Christian Anarchist draws sustenance (27, p. 406). Of course Adams qualifies the influence by saying that he "drew life from Hegel and Schopenhauer *rightly understood*" (italics mine). The apparent correlation between the philosophers and the Conservative Christian Anarchist would be this: Hegelianism is both a method and a doctrine. The method is the dialectic of thesis, antithesis, and synthesis, and this kind of method informs the movement of the six chapters. The doctrine is the resolution of contraries through dialectical negation, and a roughly analogous process occurs within the chapters. From Schopenhauer, he may have derived a concept of the inseparability of subject and object, and this implies the appropriateness of the view that he is the center of history.

Fourth, such a vision satisfies the requirements of modern science, which postulates not absolute unity but rather the tentative unity of the "larger synthesis." At any given moment, the unity offered by a temporary synthesis may be destroyed by new observations requiring the formulation of another theory. Moreover, the doctrine of science, which reduced all substances to vibrating molecules and atoms, made the apparent unity of substance equal to the multiplicity of motion. As Adams puts it, "the scientific synthesis commonly called Unity was the scientific analysis commonly called Multiplicity. The two things were the same, all forms being shifting phases of motion" (29, p. 431).

For all these reasons, the double vision of chaos and order is not only appropriate, but exceedingly ingenious—the more so if the reader recalls the artistic problem facing

Adams. On the one hand, he must create a synthesis of experience in the manner of Augustine, but with the extraordinary condition attached of making this synthesis (which implies unity) conform to scientific and historical notions of chaos. Thus the double vision fulfills the requirements of the contradictions by making unity and multiplicity coexist simultaneously; and the method of its implementation can be observed now to see where Adams succeeded, and where he failed.

The dialectical movement of chapters 27–32 alone displays this double vision of order and chaos. In "Teufelsdröckh," Adams as Conservative Christian Anarchist perches at the top of the globe to see its division into two camps, Russian and Western—a vision becoming quasi-scientific as he assigns values of inertia (positing unity) and acceleration (portending multiplicity) to each respectively. This politicoscientific vision of order and anarchy, held together by a perceiver symbolically uniting contradictory forces in the world, splits in half in the next two chapters.

In "The Height of Knowledge" (28) politics as manifested through the work of Secretary of State Hay assumes the guise of unity, and in "The Abyss of Ignorance" (29) the multiplicity of science strikes the main theme. Thus the chapter movement has been from a kind of synthesis of forces of unity and of multiplicity within the unifying vision of Adams in "Teufelsdröckh" (27) to thesis (unity: "The Height of Knowledge"—28) and antithesis (multiplicity: "The Abyss of Ignorance"—29) in the following chapters.

The next triad of chapters pretends to an even greater scientific bias, discussing all forces of unity in "Vis Inertiae" (30) and the opposing forces in "Vis Nova," (32) with an intervening chapter posing as a scientific resolution of the two forces in "The Grammar of Science" (31).

Within the chapters individually the same process occurs to justify what Adams later calls "a toss-up between anarchy and order" (34, p. 495). For the Conservative Christian Anarchist playing the role of Teufelsdröckh, the paradoxical vision goes farther than the view of a bipolar world which he achieves from his elevated post at Hammerfest; each aspect of the vision itself possesses the contradictory values of order and anarchy. Russia is identified with inertia or race, an ancient and unifying force (27, p. 409), but glimpses of the nation from a sleeping-car window juxtapose Virgin and railway, symbolically portraying the merging of the values of Virgin and dynamo and thus superimposing the forces of chaos upon the unity of a religious symbol: "From the first glimpse one caught from the sleeping-car window, in the early morning, of the Polish Jew at the accidental railway station, in all his weird horror, to the last vision of the Russian peasant, lighting his candle and kissing his ikon before the railway Virgin in the station at St. Petersburg, all was logical, conservative, Christian and anarchic" (27, p. 408). Jew versus Christian, railway versus Virgin—the contradictions prepare for the succeeding picture of the nation.

As race, Russia is also mass (p. 410), imagistically defined as "the ice-cap of Russian inertia" (p. 414); yet she is also "luminous like the salt of radium; but with a negative luminosity as though she were a substance whose energies had been sucked out—an inert residuum—with movement of pure inertia" (p. 409). A few lines later Adams asks: "The Russian people could never have changed—could they ever be changed?" (p. 409), but the image of luminosity, dispersion of mass, itself answers the question by providing for both possibilities. On the other hand, the forces of acceleration, logically leading to anarchy and defined through coal power, paradoxically appear as unity:

From Hammerfest to Cherbourg on one shore of the ocean—from Halifax to Norfolk on the other—one great empire was ruled by one great emperor—Coal . . . . Unity had gained that ground. [p. 415]

In "The Height of Knowledge" (28) Adams reproduces the same vision with less success. Seeking to contrast the effects of mechanical force which unify society politically but dissolve the personality of its leaders (Roosevelt, Lodge, and Hay), the chapter itself dissolves into a chaos of random observations, eulogizing Lodge and criticizing Roosevelt without focusing upon the theme. But even here, the simultaneous visions of order and chaos appear. Domestically, the nation dissolves into "independent centres of force" (28, p. 419) which autonomously control the men presumably in charge (p. 421); yet a contrary process toward unity emerges on the international scene as Hay and McKinley paradoxically move toward the socialist schemes of Jaures and Bebel in their system of consolidations of government (p. 423)— an astonishing discovery again suggesting the operation of blind force independent of human control.

In "The Abyss of Ignorance" (29) Adams investigates the implications of the loss of human autonomy in a world of force only to discover that the unified world of scholastic philosophy depended upon thought to imply an intelligent Prime Motor creating unity, whereas science declared that unity and multiplicity are one, and psychology followed the pattern by analyzing the personality into multiple parts. Upon this scientific identification of order and anarchy the next triad of chapters attempts to construct a synthesis resolving political and scientific concepts, an incomplete though valiant effort to unify human experience within the constructs of modern science—politics here serving as the channel through which man expresses his most concrete and active efforts to make unity a reality.

The chapters operate within the context of the impending Russo-Japanese War, a conflict which in his letters Adams saw as major because of its implications for the future of European political alignments,[24] but which, within these pages, assumes value as a measure of human inertial energies against the accelerative energies of mechanical force

[24] Ford, vol. 2, contains a wide variety of letters on the subject of the Russo-Japanese War. See especially pp. 421, 423, 424.

represented by Japan. Thus the real question underlying the crisis is whether human force can withstand the onslaught of mechanical power. "Vis Inertiae" answers the Russian question in American terms, for sexual inertia is more constant than racial, and yet mechanical force in America threatens the continuation of humanity itself. "He was studying the laws of motion, and had struck two large questions of vital importance to America— inertia of race and inertia of sex" (30, p. 444), and in both cases traditional forces associated with the Virgin and creating unity are juxtaposed against the more powerful forces of the dynamo. But the result is a wandering narrative which, in spite of interesting political implications and rather prescient sociological observations regarding the status of American women, shows no clear connection between the political and sociological realms. The real value of the chapter, which portrays rivalry between Russia and the West, apparently lies in the irony that American technological skill can possibly defeat Russian hordes, but that this very technology threatens the existence of sexual motives: "One gazed mute before this ocean of darkest ignorance that had already engulfed society" (p. 448).

Having opposed human inertia to mechanical acceleration, Adams returns in "The Grammar of Science" (31) to some of the elements already appearing in "The Abyss of Ignorance," but this time with a new sense of their meaning. The interconvertibility of matter and motion—of order and chaos—now appears as a historical turning point in the continuity of thought which, going beyond this conception, can no longer impose order upon the universe:

As far as one ventured to interpret actual science, the mind had thus far adjusted itself by an infinite series of infinitely delicate adjustments forced on it by the infinite motion of an infinite chaos of motion; dragged at one moment into the unknowable and unthinkable, then trying to scramble back within its senses and to bar the chaos out, but always assimilating bits of it, until at last, in 1900, a new avalanche of unknown forces had fallen on it, which required new mental powers to control. [31, pp. 460–61]

The Conservative Christian Anarchist, in short, has reached the ultimate limits of contradiction; as long as man's knowledge of chaos could be assimilated rationally into a coherent world view, unity could be achieved, even though man recognized the unity as an illusion only. But the avalanche of an infinite number of supersensual, unapprehendable forces threatened even the creation of illusions and thus thought, as well as an art grounded in scientific reality, reaches its limits. So, too, Adams reaches his.

In "Vis Nova" the avalanche of new force is unleashed through the Russo-Japanese War, which becomes "a measure of relative energy on the historical scale," the whole episode making "a Grammar of new Science quite as instructive as that of Pearson" (32, p. 465). Adams saw great significance in that war because of the centrality of Russia (in his view) as a possible force in future human affairs. Writing to Gaskell, he voices a sentiment repeatedly emerging through other letters over a period of more than a decade:

Russia is very rapidly foundering. At least the old Russia has got its death-blow. Either she must go to pieces, or found a new system. Every day brings a new shock to the old one. It is the greatest event that has taken place in our time, as a catastrophe, —even greater than the War of 1870 and the catastrophe of France. Really I am glad to have lived to see this old chapter closed, and want only to know whether it will end in a big tragedy like Louis XVI, or in a tragi-comedy. Never has so great an empire sunk without dragging the world down with it. The confusion will be vast.[25]

The emphasis upon the Russo-Japanese War, then, is no casual groping for a convenient symbol of conflict; it proceeds from deepest conviction. In the *Education,* the found-

[25] 22 July 1904, Ford, 2: 437–38.

ering of Russia represents the disintegration of racial (human) energies foreshadowing the worldwide triumph of mechanical forces which lead (as in "The Grammar of Science") to the very limits of contradiction which the reason can grasp, and beyond, into a world transcending the powers of reason. Adams does not go beyond. In "Vis Nova" (32, p. 468), the Virgin of Coutances is juxtaposed against the Saint Louis Exposition, a sequel to the Chicago Exposition, showing the enduring power of the dynamo. This juxtaposition represents the limits of rational contradiction, and the persona symbolically unites these as he drives in his automobile to explore the French countryside with its monuments to the Virgin.

But the assassination of de Plehve shows that the world is to go beyond into the supersensual chaos, and the news reaching him in Troyes wildly juxtaposes the work of the dynamo against the monuments of a religious age: "Martyrs, murderers, Caesars, saints and assassins—half in glass and half in telegram; chaos of time, place, morals, forces and motive—gave him vertigo" (32, p. 471). "The conservative Christian anarchist had come to his own, but which was he —the murderer or the murdered?" (p. 472). In short, the assassination brings not just Adams, but the world as well, to the limits of contradiction. The persona has been carried down through the centuries by force—first the unifying force of the Virgin, then the fracturing force of the dynamo. He has felt the power of both and, as man has moved from the control of one force to the other, he has adopted a double vision of order and chaos to show in a literary mode the relations in historical movement which he has privately verified.

The process of the chapters, then, is one of becoming. It is an experiment, but a double-headed one. Having felt the power of Virgin and dynamo, and having recognized how they might explain his private experience, Adams assigns them tentatively the scientific values of inertia and acceleration and symbolically patterns the experience of these last pages accordingly—until he reaches the limits of a process which can hold order and chaos together. But it is clear that Adams thinks of this private experiment in larger terms, and from the beginning of the adventure in "Twilight" he betrays a hope that its value will go beyond the needs of the self: "Politics and geology pointed alike to the larger synthesis of rapidly increasing complexity; but still an elderly man knew that the change might be only in himself" (36, p. 402). Of the contrary forces of Virgin and dynamo he writes: "Of the attraction he needed no proof on his own account: but as teacher he needed to speak for others than himself" (33, p. 469).

Clearly he desires that the view of history which is founded on his own needs will have educational value for others; but its truth will depend upon its predictive value, and so Adams writes the experiment out knowing that it can only be tested in time: "Past history is only a value of relation to the future, and this value is wholly one of convenience, which can be tested only by experiment" (33, p. 488). "For his dynamic theory of history he cared no more than for the kinetic theory of gas: but, if it were an approach to measurement of motion, it would verify or disprove itself within thirty years" (35, p. 501). And this educational motive is part and parcel of his scientific and literary motives, for only by perceiving the organic connections between the last section and the earlier narrative can the reader see Adams's later quest as a logical heroic effort to come to terms with his world. In the final triad of chapters, that effort is made most explicit.

In "A Dynamic Theory of History" (33) Adams presents the clues to the movement of narrative and persona in the first twenty chapters and sets that movement in a broad historical perspective. First, by focusing on Constantine's fourth-century Edict of Milan admitting Christianity as a state religion, Adams establishes an implicit analogy with the movement of the *Education* through the Civil War years.

The centralizing force of Christianity required the extension of the slavocracy in the empire until the economy was wrecked; so, too, the centralizing force of mechanical power led the South to compete by extending its slave system till it went to wreck in the Civil War. Second, by seeing the movement between the twelfth century and his own time as a tug of war between natural force and theological, Adams explains the movement of his own persona as he repeatedly turns from the present to the past in subjective moments of experience.

"A Law of Acceleration" (34) relates to the last section of the *Education*. There Adams attempts to synthesize an ever growing body of knowledge by observing forces of order and of anarchy and by molding them into a single vision— a dialectic which posits anarchy within order, which sees unity as an illusion concealing chaos and simultaneously accounts for apparent order within disorder. Adams reaches the limits of this dialectic with the advent of supersensual forces, and the chapter on "Law" images the process in the form of a comet ready to explode.

With this scientific theory explicitly formulated, "Nunc Age" (35) concludes the *Education* by imagistically rendering the advent of man's final (ethereal) stage of existence ("The cylinder had exploded, and thrown great masses of stone and steam against the sky" [35, p. 499]), and by comparing the world scene to Rome shortly before the fall ("For the first time in fifteen hundred years a true Roman *pax* was in sight" [35, p. 503]). The reader recalls the chapters immediately preceding and perceives a scientific fatalism blending with Adams's vision of the new world, of the new phase dawning as Adams himself departs from history; and a special urgency attends the ironic injunction to act. The artistry is complete, integrating the scientific vision of force and phase with the educational motive, gently telling the reader that his education must begin where Adams's leaves off, in the age of supersensual chaos.

4

The Essential Education of Henry Adams:

The Idea of History in the *Chartres* and the *Education*

The Adams Heritage and Eighteenth-Century Assumptions

Just as critics no longer interpret Henry Adams's stance of failure literally, but find in it a mask for the social critic and philosopher, so too it is time to refrain from pointing out the absurdity of Adams's attempt to wed history with the physical sciences and to ask why such a gifted mind turned in this direction. If the answer is to be significant, it must go beyond the simple observation that Adams lived in a milieu profoundly affected by science, and that he was affected by Buckle, Spencer, and Comte. This is true, and this explains why the *Education* is so congenial to modern readers. They may reject as a nineteenth-century curio his literal scientific goals, but they find in the blossoming disciplines of our own day—sociology, political science, and psychology—much of the subject matter of Adams's book systematized by scientific method, if not by the physical laws of nature. The methods of these disciplines may not be those of the chemist or physicist, but some are designed to establish social laws, if not physical ones.

There is another sense in which Adams's science is important—a sense which emphasizes neither the goal nor the achievement as it is found in his three versions of the dynamic theory but rather the motives for the quest. Here the *Education* is an important document. If the book contains a manikin, an account of society, and a theory of history, it is also a record of the logic leading Adams to scientific history. And just as its artistry cannot be appreciated independent of his later scientific theories, so too the entire logic of the book leads to that theorizing. As the record of a quest, this is self-evident if Adams is seen as a mere hunter after certainty and predictability in history, for these elements are what we expect from science. But to isolate this aspect of his search from other motives prompting it is to classify him as an eccentric or to shelve him as a thing of the past. It was not so much his desire for immutable principles as his criticism of an age and a self which thought it possessed them that drove him to science and scientific history. Although the *Education* concludes with highly problematic solutions to a historical puzzle, the bulk of the book is concerned with the problematic character of the "eternal verities" which constitute Adams's heritage—and ours—and the nature of those presumed truths led Adams to science, precisely because they were based on a scientific view of the world.[1]

The last chapter showed that the book possesses an artistic coherence leading to Adams's later notions of history. In order to show that its subject matter possesses a logical coherence leading to the same theorizing, it is necessary to understand exactly what Adams means by education. Carl Becker has pointed to a double use of the term in the *Education,* meaning both the tools necessary to acquire an effective grasp of his world and the underlying agencies, mysterious in nature, which guide that world.[2] Thus Adams's stated need for a mastery of mathematics, French,

[1] Howard M. Munford would agree. See his "Henry Adams and the Tendency of History," *New England Quarterly* 32 (March 1959): 79–90. Also see his "Henry Adams: The Limitations of Science," *Southern Review* 4 (1968): n.s. 59–71. In the more recent article he observes that Adams found science highly subjective.

[2] "The Education of Henry Adams," *American Historical Review* 24 (April 1919): 422–34. Reprinted in *Every Man His Own Historian* (New York, 1935), pp. 143–61.

German, and Spanish would represent education in the first sense, whereas his desire to make history a predictable science illustrates the second meaning of the term. But there is another way of looking at its meaning which gives the book its most modern character, which represents its most fascinating quality.

Despite repeated assertions to the contrary, the reader of the *Education* clearly knows that the young Adams does receive an education. Although the book is never precise about the term, it contains frequent references to the fact that he was in the process of getting, and did attain, an eighteenth-century education. The term "eighteenth-century" carries pejorative overtones, insofar as it renders Henry Adams unfit to cope with the modern world. Because he always characterizes his education as "eighteenth-century," and because this description is offered as the reason for his failure to cope with the modern world, it seems clear that by education Adams means the frame of reference of an epoch through which man organizes his past experience intelligibly, and within which he learns to order new experience and gain new knowledge. The basis of his education would then be what Alfred North Whitehead later called those "fundamental assumptions which adherents of all the variant systems within . . . an epoch consciously presuppose. Such assumptions appear so obvious that people do not know what they are assuming because no other way of putting things has ever occurred to them."[3]

Adams surely is using education in this sense, for it explains why Quincy and the South—at least the eighteenth-century South—became identical in his consciousness. "Mount Vernon," recall, "was only Quincy in a Southern setting. No doubt it was much more charming, but it was the same eighteenth-century, the same old furniture, the

[3] Alfred North Whitehead, *Science and the Modern World* (New York, 1941), p. 71.

same old patriot, and the same old President" (3, p. 48).
How could Quincy have anything in common with the
South? Quincy is unalterably opposed to slavery, while the
South is a slavocracy. The answer is that both the slave
power and Quincy once shared the same fundamental as-
sumptions.

This idea lies behind the symbolism of George Washington and Mount Vernon, contained in that famous observation from the *Education:*

George Washington could not be reached on Boston lines. George
Washington was a primary, or, if Virginians liked it better, an
ultimate relation like the Pole Star, and amid the endless restless
motion of every other visible point in space, he alone remained
steady, in the mind of Henry Adams, to the end. All the other
points shifted their bearings; John Adams, Jefferson, Madison,
Franklin, even John Marshall, took varied lights, and assumed
new relations, but Mount Vernon always remained where it was,
with no practicable road to reach it. [3, pp. 47–48]

Mount Vernon thus symbolizes the fundamental, un-
questioned assumptions presupposed by "adherents of all
the variant systems" within the eighteenth century—to use
Whitehead's phrase. These assumptions are exposed as
fallacies in the next century when they give rise to contradictions. Adams alludes to one of these when, after describing
his visit to Mount Vernon, he writes that "he never thought
to ask himself or his father how to deal with the moral
problem that deduced George Washington from the sum of
all wickedness" (3, p. 48). The existence of such contradictions indicates that assumptions must be reexamined and
perhaps discarded in favor of new ones which will create a
new conceptual framework of thought removing the
contradictions.

The education of Henry Adams consists in his abandon-
ment of such an eighteenth-century framework and his
heroic effort to construct a twentieth-century one. Between

the two poles lay a long period of confusion, taking the form of paradox, each one a memento mori of the eighteenth century. Some of these paradoxes, like the disappearance of religion and a vital art, or the unsexing of women, also act as poignant reminders of the lost world of the *Chartres;* but because the structure of the *Education* identifies the eighteenth century as the tail end of a religious era in history, such paradoxes recall this later time as well. More particularly, they point to an eighteenth-century *America.* The *Education* has as its fulcrum the Civil War, a dividing line between an old and a new America which Adams cannot bridge with a mere sequence of facts, because these facts pointed to paradox, not change alone. After his return from diplomatic service abroad, he continually specifies this distinction between a new, capitalist America, where neither the moral law nor the Constitution prevailed, and the simpler nation familiar to him in childhood and known intimately by John Quincy Adams. "Had they been Tyrian traders of the year B.C. 1000, landing from a galley fresh from Gibraltar, they could hardly have been stranger on the shore of a world, so changed from what it had been ten years before" (16, p. 237).

That events of American history should become his center for paradox is hardly surprising. It would be more astonishing if the descendant of ancestors distinguished for their role in American life had moved his central focus elsewhere. Nor is it at all amazing that he should discover paradox where others saw only change. Within his consciousness he carried the convictions of the eighteenth century passed on to him by his forebears. Those convictions, always centered upon American experience, he deemed immutable truths. But if they were immutable, the post–Civil War world could never have arisen; or else man, in his sheer perversity, once again demonstrated his capacity for evil and wilfully violated eternal laws. In his experience as reformer Adams became convinced that the latter was not true; and so the changes in American life which troubled him emerged in his consciousness as paradoxes which could not be explained by a sequence of facts, precisely because that sequence, describing change, did not follow from eighteenth-century premises. Instead, those paradoxes pointed to a need for reinvestigating basic premises, together with the construction of new ones to impart meaning to life in the twentieth century. But no matter in which direction he looked, past or future, toward the demolition of old assumptions or the acceptance of new ones, science necessarily played a leading role.

In his splendid introductory essay, "The Heritage of Henry Adams," Brooks Adams suggested how basic science was to the fundamental assumptions of his grandfather, John Quincy Adams, and how the grandfather's scientific interests provided a context within which to read and understand Henry Adams's scientific essays, first published together in the posthumous volume entitled *The Degradation of the Democratic Dogma.* In his introduction Brooks Adams showed that his brother Henry's interest in science derived from their grandfather; that John Quincy believed science provided the clue to an understanding of the destiny of the American republic; that the grandfather's life ended in despair because the events of American history, within his own lifetime, flagrantly violated the expectations of the old man, particularly as these hopes were related to science; and that the grandson then returned to science, the source of his grandfather's basic assumptions, in order to correct them and to explain coherently the progress of American history both within John Quincy's lifetime and within his own.[4]

The essay is particularly illuminating because of its special angle of vision. By demonstrating that science was the groundwork for many of John Quincy Adams's social and political convictions, Brooks emphasized that their validity

[4] *Degradation,* pp. 1–36.

was put to the test by the events of American history. Thus Henry Adams of the *Education* follows a family tradition, for there he views American experience in the same way, adopting as unquestionable truths the beliefs of a grandfather who symbolized "the eighteenth century, as an actual and living companion" (1, p. 20).

The convictions of John Quincy Adams smack of naïve Enlightenment views of man's perfectibility, although his political practice had a modern, congenial air. Brooks Adams described the relation between theory and practice in a way which would not set his grandfather very far apart from most eighteenth-century rationalists:

> Mr. Adams as a scientific man was a precursor of the later Darwinians who have preached the doctrine of human perfectibility, a doctrine in which the modern world has believed and still professes to believe. Granting that there is a benign and omnipotent Creator of the world, who watches over the fate of men, Adams's sincere conviction was that such a being thinks according to certain fixed laws, which we call scientific laws; that these laws may be discovered by human intelligence and when discovered may be adapted to human uses. And if so discovered, adapted, and practised they must lead men certainly to an approach to perfection, and more especially to the elimination of war and slavery. The theory was pleasing, and since the time of Mr. Adams it has been generally accepted as the foundation of American education and the corner stone of democracy.[5]

This description involves two fundamental assumptions: that there is a God who has established a mechanical harmony in the universe, and that an adaptation of its laws can lead men to perfection—two assumptions obviously shared by Henry Adams of the *Education,* where a struggling young man follows the same optimistic notions of his grandfather and for a short time becomes a nineteenth-century Darwinian, replacing God with a belief in natural selection but

[5] Ibid., pp. 30–31.

sustaining his hopes for a heaven on earth. For both men, science held promising social implications.

Both grandfather and grandson saw their convictions fail, Henry in the dry light of the Grant administration, John Quincy in his defeat by Jackson in the election of 1828. John Quincy Adams fervently desired to adapt nature to man's best uses. For the grandfather, government's proper concerns were internal improvements and the conservation of the public lands so that the fruits of science, the steam engine and modern industry, could become the nation's economic source of unity, ultimately extirpating the moral evil of slavery and elevating and purifying the people as a whole. The possibilities of such a government vanished in Jackson's triumph, when he began his great giveaway of public lands. And science itself, which John Quincy Adams believed would provide an industrial base eliminating the need for slavery, instead gave rise to the cotton gin, consolidated slavery, and ultimately led to the Civil War which the old man foresaw years before his death. For grandfather and grandson, therefore, the assumptions of perfectibility were shattered by the facts of succeeding American experience. But there is a significant difference between the two. Whereas John Quincy lapsed into the despair of near atheism, Henry Adams questioned more than perfectibility; he went beyond to question the source of that optimism, the mechanical universe of science.

It is in this regard that Brooks Adams's introductory essay is least helpful. Although he provides an illuminating framework for the scientific essays, Brooks largely ignores Henry Adams's *Education* as an account of the broader logic leading his brother to science and as a dramatic rendering of the solution to the discrepancy between theory and American experience which its author intended. The paradoxes of the *Education* were, for Brooks, typical of the lighter side of his brother's character. "I think in his 'Education' he has carried his joke, at times, perhaps a little too far for his own fame."[6] Distinguishing between the sobriety of the essays and the frivolity of the *Education,* Brooks thought of his introduction as a corrective, a "counterpoise, as it were, to his 'Education,' where he has loved to dilate on what he thought more amusing."[7]

This is no condemnation of Brooks Adams. "To begin with," Brooks wrote, "Henry was never, I fear, quite frank with himself or with others; certainly he was not with me."[8] He added, "Nor was I ever myself quite sure how much he believed in his own paradoxes."[9] Henry Adams was a difficult man to know. Even with his brother, "even with me, Henry was always shy and oversensitive and disliked disagreeable subjects. Hence he would surround himself with different defences, all of them calculated to repel tactless advances, and on these defences few of us cared to intrude. Personally I at least, always avoided them."[10] It is easy to see that the world of the *Education,* with its paradoxes, its failures, its apparent despair, might easily be construed by Brooks (who was himself a notorious hypochondriac)[11] as a series of neurotic maneuvers by an overscrupulous and oversensitive mind. Besides, nearness sometimes clouds vision. But the point remains that this family interest which Brooks insisted was fundamental to an understanding of Henry Adams's scientific essays can also alert the reader to the fundamental issue of the *Education.*

Although Brooks Adams emphasized the importance of the events of American history in testing the assumptions of his grandfather and his brother, it is likely, given the special

[6] Ibid., p. 6.
[7] Ibid., p. 7.
[8] Ibid., p. 1.
[9] Ibid., p. 4.
[10] Ibid., pp. 1–2.
[11] See Arthur F. Beringause, *Brooks Adams: A Biography* (New York, 1955), pp. 153–54.

use of the term "eighteenth century" in the *Education,* that Henry Adams was investigating a broader framework of assumptions which led to the nation's founding. The theme of his novel *Democracy,* which critics agree is a foreshadowing of the *Education,* displays this concern with a movement away from the original principles on which America was based,[12] just as the *Education* does. The artistic structure of the *Education* portrays Quincy, and hence eighteenth-century America, as a degraded relic of a religious era; and in this way the structure denies that brave new beginning which popular thought ascribed to the American Revolution. Furthermore, the values behind Mount Vernon and George Washington, both of which are polar stars in Henry Adams's thought within the book, confirm an interest in the principles leading to the creation of the nation. Hence the belief in perfectibility, as Brooks defined it, must be adapted to a larger framework of assumptions contributing to America's founding; Brooks Adams simply tied it to John Quincy Adams's political support of a system of internal improvements carried out under the auspices of the central government.

John Quincy Adams's own words can provide the reader with the key concept guiding the eighteenth-century framework of Henry Adams's thought within the *Education.* In an Independence Day address delivered at Quincy seven years before the birth of Henry Adams, the grandfather announced to his fellow townsmen a concept of American history which was not his alone but would have been adhered to by all the fathers of the country and by most of the major leaders of the Enlightenment. "In the history of the world," he said, "this was the first example of a self-constituted nation proclaiming to the rest of mankind the principles upon which it was associated, and deriving those

---

[12] See especially chapter 6, with its setting at Mount Vernon.

principles from the laws of nature."[13] The meaning of nature
to the eighteenth century, and the expression of this meaning
in literature, philosophy, and political thought are problems
which clearly go beyond the resources or aims of this analysis. But given Henry Adams's center, America's founding,
and given his broad meaning for education, those fundamental assumptions presupposed by "adherents of all the
variant systems," one can make a few points, already established by scholars and of demonstrable interest to Henry
Adams, to show the intricacies of pattern in his *Education*.

John Quincy Adams's words clearly refer to the natural
law of philosophy, with its attendant conception of natural
rights, embodied in the Declaration of Independence and
expressing the guiding principles of American national life.
The date of this speech, Independence Day, proves this. This
was no speech designed to offer mere lip service to principle.
John Quincy Adams did not so indulge. George Lipsky, who
wrote a most thorough study of his theory and ideas, states,
"On all appropriate occasions Adams asserted the principles of the Declaration in his contest with his political
enemies."[14] But the document was useful in more than
political warfare and played an essential role in John
Quincy's political theory:

> Adams held, in effect, that the Declaration was as much a part
> of the public law of the land as the Constitution, that it had estab-
> lished the proper relations among the states in the federal rela-
> tionship, that the Constitution was the final fruition of the
> political evolution set in motion by the Declaration.[15]

Precisely because America was founded on these "laws of

[13] "An Oration Addressed to the Citizens of the Town of Quincy
on the Fourth of July, 1831, the Fifty Fifth Anniversary of the Independence of the United States of America," *Slavery Pamphlets* (Boston,
1831), 22: 18.

[14] *John Quincy Adams, His Theory and Ideas* (New York, 1950),
p. 212.

[15] Lipsky, p. 212.

nature," therefore, it was, from the Adams point of view, unique in the history of the world. The Declaration was the harbinger of a new era in the life of nations.

Carl Becker, that student of the climate of opinion of the eighteenth century, has observed, "Not all Americans, it is true, would have accepted the philosophy of the Declaration, just as Jefferson phrased it, without qualification, as the 'common sense of the subject'; but one may say that the premises of this philosophy, the underlying preconceptions from which it is derived, were commonly taken for granted."[16] Those premises were what Becker called the assumptions of the eighteenth century. John Adams wrote of the Declaration that "There is not an idea in it but what had been hackneyed in Congress for two years before,"[17] and Jefferson readily agreed, adding, as if to answer latent criticism for lack of originality, "I did not consider it as any part of my charge to invent new ideas altogether and to offer no sentiment which had ever been expressed before."[18] Becker shows that this natural-law philosophy attracted adherents of many variant systems in the eighteenth century;[19] at the very least, no matter how widely divergent the interpretation of natural law, the concept drew together the rival political ideologies of Jefferson and John Adams in America; it maintained the support of John Quincy Adams, and the underlying preconceptions sustaining it thus play an important role in the heritage of Henry Adams.

[16] *The Declaration of Independence: A Study in the History of Political Ideas* (New York, 1940), p. 26. In this and the following two paragraphs I am indebted to Becker, chapter 2, "Historical Antecedents of the Declaration: The Natural Rights Philosophy," pp. 24–79.

[17] From the *Works of John Adams*, 2: 512. Quoted by Becker, p. 24.

[18] From *The Writings of Thomas Jefferson* (Ed. 1869), 7: 304. Quoted by Becker, p. 25.

[19] Becker shows that the natural-law philosophy was used as a support for revelation by English and American divines (see pp. 76 ff.) and as a sustitute for revelation by figures like Jefferson and Rousseau (p. 36).

The idea of natural law was not an eighteenth-century invention. Ancient Greeks and Romans appealed to the concept in their philosophy and law. Thomas Aquinas made use of it. From the Renaissance on it became progressively more popular until it became the basis for a political philosophy which the founding fathers derived mainly from John Locke. It was a broad term and had many meanings, but the basic concept insisted upon the existence of a law higher than the state—a law universally valid and discoverable only by reason—and in this sense the concept had not altered radically through the ages.[20] By the time of Locke, however, modern science had gained enough power over the minds of men to give the concept of natural law an authority and a meaning justifying the American Revolution with its attendant principles as formulated in the Declaration of Independence.

Natural law, of course, was not identifiable with the physical laws of science as Copernicus, Kepler, Galileo, and (most importantly) Newton had been formulating them. But for the age of Newton, the inductive method of science had so promised to reveal the mechanism of the physical world that, as Carl Becker has observed, "the Newtonian philosophy became a 'Philosophy' indeed."[21] Rather than looking to a God disclosed in revelation, the eighteenth-century man thought the divine mind could be known through the physical laws of nature. It was this view of God which Brooks Adams characterized his grandfather as holding, and as a view it provided a natural-law philosophy with special strength. Just as man could know the physical laws of nature inductively, without recourse to a priori hypotheses (remember Newton's famous statement, "I frame no hypotheses; for whatever is not deduced from the phae-

[20] My phrasing is indebted to Dagobert D. Runes, *Dictionary of Philosophy* (New York, 1942), p. 206.
[21] Becker, p. 47.

nomena is to be called an hypothesis."[22]), so the nature of man and the kind of government under which he should live could be similarly arrived at by analyzing natural laws governing men—laws whose existence was presumed to be as objective as the physical laws of nature discovered by the scientist. And the observance of these natural laws could bring society into the harmony discoverable in physical nature.[23]

There is an obvious contradiction here, since the scientist derived his physical laws of nature empirically from the observation of the material objects in the universe, whereas the natural-law philosophy postulated the objective existence of its own law and then derived from it the proper nature of government; but this was the contradiction of an age. Before exploring the inconsistency further, it is necessary to elaborate the fundamental assumptions of this age to see how they relate to the founding of America, and finally to the problem of education for Henry Adams.

The tradition of Bacon, Galileo, and Newton specified the use of an inductive method to define the physical laws of the universe. Thus revelation and a priori hypotheses were replaced by experimentation, a method which does not try to fit the operation of phenomena into a preconceived view of the universe. This is what Henry Adams means in the *Education* when he writes of Lord Bacon: "He urged society to lay aside the idea of evolving the universe from a thought, and to try evolving thought from the universe" (31, p. 484). This scientific method necessarily entailed, as one philosopher put it, the possibility of having "a correct

[22] *Mathematical Principles of Natural Philosophy,* Book 3.

[23] In chapter 2 Becker shows that the Newtonian science animated many men to bring society into the harmony of nature; that Locke's theory of ideas, allowing for a rejection of the past, strengthened this possibility; and that the method of implementing such harmony was through an adherence to the natural rights philosophy, particularly as Locke formulated it.

knowledge of the part without knowing the nature of the whole,"[24] and this aspect of science in the eighteenth century interested Henry Adams enough to make him exclaim, in the *Education,* "Neither Galileo nor Kepler, neither Spinoza nor Descartes, neither Leibnitz nor Newton . . . doubted Unity" (33, p. 484). When Henry Adams turned to science in his later years, he found that a universe which could be reduced to a single set of laws, the mechanical universe of Newton, was indeed in doubt. But even Newton himself only assumed that unity, never asserting its existence until proved. Hence, from either point of view, from Adams's later skepticism or Newton's empirical method, science admitted as an assumption what was taken to be a fact by the eighteenth-century mind—John Quincy Adams, for one, according to the testimony of Brooks Adams. *The physical world is a harmony.*

The assumption of science reached and affected popular thought radically. Alexander Pope, whose poetic goal was to enshrine in couplets "What oft was thought, but ne'er so well expressed," could write confidently of the new universe: "A mighty maze! but not without a plan." And just as the inductive method of science could reveal the complete harmony of nature, so man must study himself inductively, freed from the errors or assumptions of the past. "Know then thyself, presume not God to scan / The proper study of Mankind is Man," advised Pope,[25] a faith served perfectly by Locke's *Two Treatises on Government.*

[24] Roland Van Zandt, *Metaphysical Foundations of American History* (The Hague, 1959), p. 15. With a purpose different from mine (he point to a need for American historians to develop a philosophy of history) Van Zandt shows how America became a vindication of a new point of view deriving from Newton and the philosophical tradition following him. The two assumptions of the eighteenth-century mind which I employ later are similar to those he uses, though he applies them to Jefferson's thought. He repeats them in a variety of ways in his book. See especially pp. 69–70, 86–87, 123–24, 205–23.

[25] *Essay on Criticism,* 1.298; *Essay on Man,* 1. 1.6; 2. 11.1–2.

The story need not be repeated at great length. It is well known. Basing his arguments upon the existence of a natural law "as intelligible and plain to a rational Creature, and a Studier of that Law, as the positive Laws of Commonwealths, nay possibly plainer,"[26] Locke espoused the doctrine of natural rights which became the substance of the Declaration of Independence; the theory of government as a voluntary compact between the people and the state and subject to dissolution—a theory which justified the American Revolution; and the system of government based on the separation of powers to guarantee the self-evident freedom of every individual, which was a predominant influence in the making of the American Constitution. Hence American democracy became, in the words of F. S. C. Northrop,

a method subject to constitutional limitations which are defined by and which presuppose a specific theory of the nature of the individual and of the relation of the state and private property to that individual—the specific theory in fact which was formulated by John Locke.[27]

Through the implementation of this philosophy, whose popularity was generated by the strong movements in science, the second fundamental assumption of eighteenth-century thought, particularly as it concerns America, follows: *America is the political expression of the harmony in physical nature.* This is so because its fundamental principles, written in the Declaration, and its political structure formulated in the Constitution, are the realization of a philosophy of natural law specifying that, through its observance, man can "correspond with the general harmony of Nature"[28] observed in the physical world. To secure that

[26] *Two Treatises of Government*, book 2.

[27] *The Meeting of East and West: An Inquiry concerning World Understanding* (New York, 1946), p. 97.

[28] Becker, p. 57. Becker quotes the phrase from Colin Maclaurin's *An Account of Sir Isaac Newton's Philosophical Discoveries*. Earlier he discusses Maclaurin to show how, even in the mind of Newton's

harmony in society was the goal of John Quincy Adams, who frequently invoked the doctrine of natural law to support his stand for internal improvements, and whose Independence Day address at Quincy related America's uniqueness to its self-constituted existence as an embodiment of that law.

Given these two principles, that the physical world is a harmony and that America became the expression of that harmony by adopting a natural law philosophy as its social and political inspiration, a third follows: If the future course of the nation went astray, it was not because the philosophical tenets were wrong, for in the Enlightenment mind they were as objective as, and were given support by, Newtonian science. Rather, *man himself was morally culpable for violating these laws.* Whether or not this final principle was in the eighteenth-century air, the stubborn resistance of Henry Adams to abandoning his eighteenth-century inheritance in the *Education* suggests that this reasoning was valid, for him at least; and not surprisingly, since he was trapped in the great contradiction of the age.

What George Lipsky wrote of John Quincy Adams could have applied to many of those admirers of science who also adhered to a natural rights philosophy:

> Adams's life was one of inquiry and inspection of the causes of things in the realm of science, wherein his method, in the manner of Locke, was empirical and rejected large generalizations and *a priori* affirmations. But just as clearly as Locke, through failure to inspect first principles, he saw no contradiction between his empiricism, on the one hand, and his natural law, natural rights doctrine, on the other.[29]

The comparison is a telling one, for Locke, the single greatest influence on American political thought, shows this

---

major scientific disciple, the science inspired "a general philosophy of the universe." See pp. 49–51.

[29] Lipsky, pp. 72–73.

inconsistency between an avowed empiricism and a sharp departure from it nowhere more than in his most famous works, the *Essay concerning Human Understanding* and the *Two Treatises on Government*. The *Essay* shows its indebtedness to the empirical methods of science by rejecting innate ideas as the source of human knowledge (just as science rejected hypotheses and allowed the observable phenomena to induce generalizations in the inquiring scientist). Furthermore, in a universe composed only of mental substances and material ones, so far as science could verify empirically, Locke constructed his famous theory of the tabula rasa accordingly; the mind gains all ideas from its interaction with matter, whether the simple ideas, which are mere sense data, or more complex ones, which are associations of sense data. On this foundation he built his theory of the limitations of the understanding.[30]

The *Two Treatises* were another story. Evidently Locke was aware that his insistence upon the objective reality of natural laws guiding man's conduct conflicted with his empiricism, but he steadfastly refused to allow that these laws might be either innate ideas or identifiable with the variable laws of commonwealths. Although one defense of these inconsistencies shows that Locke never wrote the works as part of a body of consistent philosophy, it admits that posterity took them as corollaries.[31] The empiricism of

[30] A fine account of how Locke's theory of ideas was inspired by Newton's science is in Northrop, pp. 83 ff. He also specifies a relationship between the Newtonian science and Locke's political theory. See especially pp. 93–102. This entire third chapter, "The Free Culture of the United States," is a study of the relationships between Newtonian science and Lockean theory (of ideas and of government) and of their expression in the political and cultural life of America.

[31] Introduction to John Locke's *Two Treatises of Government*, ed. Peter Laslett (Cambridge at the University Press, 1960), p. 82. His entire Introduction, and particularly section 2, "Locke the Philosopher and Locke the Political Theorist," in which Laslett compares the *Essay* to the *Two Treatises* (pp. 79–91), is illuminating.

John Quincy Adams, together with his emphasis upon natural rights and laws, displays the same vein of inconsistency. In another way, this inconsistency became part of the fundamental pattern of paradox and self-questioning in *The Education of Henry Adams*.

The *Education* as an Expression of Eighteenth-Century Assumptions

Precisely because the events of the book are "autobiographical," much of *The Education of Henry Adams* obviously touches upon important events in American history. Given his family background, the protagonist, despite his complaints that he never really controlled power, was always near the center of power, and that center usually involved America directly. But there is a difference between the events of and the issue of American history; and it is American history as an issue which must be seen as the vital fabric of Adams's education. Like Madeleine Lee in *Democracy,* the Henry Adams of the *Education* found in the nation's capital a center of power and force proliferating throughout the country. But unlike Mrs. Lee, he discovered that these forces were not contained within national borders but penetrated beyond to the outermost reaches of the planet.

The preceding chapter of this analysis displays the artistic process of equivalences and correspondences in the *Education* whereby America becomes a symbol of the historic process itself. Now we can see further significance in that artistry. Therefore it is necessary to demonstrate that those eighteenth-century assumptions mentioned earlier pose the chief problem of the *Education,* and so it will be well to review them.

The essential elements underlying the conception of America's founding and comprising the eighteenth-century mentality of Henry Adams in the *Education* are three. First, the physical world is a harmony. Second, America began a new course in history by becoming the political expression of this harmony, because its theory of man and its political structure were based on a philosophy of natural law believed capable of bringing man into a correspondence with the harmony of the physical world. Third, because the natural laws to which Locke and the *Declaration* appealed were as objective as the physical laws of nature, and because the existence of these natural laws was given support in the Enlightenment mind by the discovery of physical laws, then if the American future did not usher in a millennium, neither the philosophical principles nor the scientific laws which gave them popular support were wrong. These both existed objectively. Instead, man was himself morally culpable for resisting eternal truths.

In short, the founding of America vindicated a world view, and one not too far removed from medieval scholasticism. At least each discovered a harmony existing in several spheres of the universe—man, nature, and God— though admittedly the character of each harmony differed greatly, owing to the medieval emphasis upon revelation and God and the eighteenth-century emphasis upon nature.[32] Despite such divergences Henry Adams was interested in the fundamental similarity, the mode of vision connecting the harmony of society with a larger harmony, a view of life still prevailing in the world of Locke as in that of Aquinas. Hence in the *Education,* when he observes the alarm of the church at the progress of modern science, Adams declares that none of these scientists doubted unity: "The utmost range of their heresies reached only its personality" (33, p. 484). And in the first paragraph of "A Letter to American Teachers of History," Adams called the mechanical theory of the universe the direct successor to a "theological scheme

[32] Becker, in *Declaration,* perceives a similarity between the thirteenth and the eighteenth century's understanding of natural law (pp. 60–61).

existing as a Unity by the will of an infinite and eternal Creator," thus stressing the likeness between the ages of God and the ages of science when Newton reigned supreme.

This point is tremendously important. It explains why the first major paradox of the *Education,* the Civil War, is not so much a test of the philosophical principles of natural law inspiring the nation, or of the obvious contradiction between the empiricism of science and the a priori assumptions of the natural law philosophy, as it is a test of the assumption that the physical world is indeed a harmony. Of course it is these other things too, as Henry Adams makes apparent through large statements such as, "The moral law had expired, like the Constitution!" or "The system of 1789 had broken down, and with it the eighteenth-century fabric of a priori, or moral, principles" (18, pp. 280–81). But it was more logical to make the Civil War a test of physical harmony in the universe, because the eighteenth-century mind, like the medieval, still operated on this assumption of a harmony existing in several spheres of the universe—at least as Adams saw the eighteenth century. In a book overthrowing an eighteenth-century world view, then, the Civil War, seen through the eyes of an eighteenth-century young man, necessarily takes on this larger value of questioning the structure of the universe.

That this was so for Henry Adams is apparent from the artistic structure of the book which, as demonstrated earlier, makes the Civil War an example of the operation of phase with its attendant consequences. Quincy and the South, whose representatives in "Harvard College" are Adams and Rooney Lee, are portrayed as competing energies, both of which are ultimately destroyed in the aftermath of the war. Hence the war tests that corollary of a Newtonian universe, the Law of the Conservation of Energy, which at the beginning of his "Letter to American Teachers of History" Henry Adams set up in direct opposition to Kelvin's Second Law, whose historical operations occupy the rest of the essay.

Since the Civil War necessarily tests the validity of a Newtonian harmony, therefore, the underlying assumptions of Adams's eighteenth-century mentality may be simplified: The physical universe is a harmony; America is an expression of that harmony; and, if American life is not harmonious, man must be at fault, because American principles are scientifically grounded.

It is into this kind of world that Henry Adams of the *Education* is born, and within its milieu the emphasis upon sensory experience in the first chapter ("Quincy") must be evaluated. This is a book about education, and education presumably leads to knowledge. How truly eighteenth-century Adams's education is can be seen by the fact that its beginnings are founded in sense impressions. Recall that the senses of color, taste, and pain were the first to educate the child (1, p. 5). Here is a Lockean world denying the existence of innate ideas, categories, and moral principles and insisting upon the mind as a tabula rasa whose edifice of knowledge will be constructed from sense experience. By this implicit reference to the supreme authority of the eighteenth century in his empirical vein, Adams summons up the empiricism of science and the first assumption of the eighteenth century, that the physical world is a harmony, and even this assumption is made explicit by the manipulation of sense impressions.

All the boy's impressions reduce themselves to the sharp contrasts of polar opposites, so that life becomes a vision of blacks and whites, and the seasonal polarity of winter and summer subsumes all the other sensory dichotomies:

The bearing of the two seasons on the education of Henry Adams was no fancy; it was the most decisive force he ever knew; it ran through life, and made the division between its perplexing, warring, irreconcilable problems, irreducible opposites, with growing emphasis to the last year of study. [1, p. 9]

These dichotomies of sense impression contain within them

no principle of harmony. But within the world of Quincy, that harmony is simply assumed. It is still a theistic world where God has imposed harmony in nature, and the evidence of the senses, which show winter and summer as ever returning cycles of nature, seems at least to confirm a principle of balance. A vital question for education, then, is to what extent the senses can be trusted. This is the very heart of eighteenth-century education, which, following Locke, insists that all knowledge is built upon them. It is for this reason that Adams can complain, "The children reached manhood without knowing religion, and with the certainty that dogma, metaphysics, and abstract philosophy were not worth knowing" (2, p. 35). Locke's denial of innate ideas, categories, and moral principles created in the eighteenth-century mind a profound distrust of these forms of knowledge because they relied on a priori assumptions. According to the evidence of the senses, then, the seasonal dichotomies possess an apparent balance, and it is therefore not surprising that Quincy should extend this principle, so evident to the senses, to its entire vision of life.

That vision is Lockean, and it is presented as peculiarly American. "So one-sided an education could have been possible in no other country or time, but it became, almost of necessity, the more literary and political" (2, p. 35). Lockean philosophy thus is best imaged in the American political structure, which is assumed to be an analogue of the natural order. Hence Boston and the South are represented as forces quite as antithetical as winter and summer, while Quincy, like the God of a mechanical universe, acts as the center of harmony to hold them in balance. The intense emphasis upon the principle of balance prevailing in the character of Charles Francis Adams (2, p. 28) and his careful attention to that principle in political life (7, p. 105) is also significant as a fundamental precept of eighteenth-century thought; it is the political expression of a view inspired by science: that it is possible for man to implement the harmony of the natural world through the special institutions of American life. What is vital in the early pages of the *Education* is that the polarities of sectional interests are an analogue of the polarities of the boy's sensory impressions. The assumed balance in nature thus will be tested within the American political scheme itself.

In this way, the Civil War becomes a test of two principal tenets of the eighteenth-century world view: that the physical world is a harmony, and that America began a new course in history by becoming the political expression of this scientific "fact." But the third element of this view denies that the Civil War can really be such a test of the first two tenets; for it insists that, because the American political structure is derived from a science finding harmony in nature, any departure from the norm can only be explained as man's immorality. This view is an important strand of the early education of Henry Adams, one which persistently hamstrings him until he sees that the principles themselves are in fact not valid.

This last view is the view of the moralist, and it begins the book. At his grandfather's funeral, thus, the boy recalls how Adams principles conflict with the commercialism of the Hartford Convention and the immorality of the slavocracy (1, p. 21); but he overcomes his uneasiness by settling for self-righteous morality rather than by questioning first principles. "Even then he felt that something was wrong, but he concluded that it must be Boston. Quincy had always been right, for Quincy represented a moral principle—the principle of resistance to Boston" (1, p. 21). Of course one cannot expect a boy of ten to question first principles, but Adams's trouble is that it takes him so long to outgrow his morality. Throughout his stay in England during the Civil War he was forever "seeking a moral standard for judging politicians" (10, p. 152). The central chapter of the four dealing with diplomatic negotiations is called "Political Morality" (10), thus emphasizing the importance of a theme which becomes the focus for all his speculations on the maneuvers of English politicians. Although he is probably poking some fun at himself, this emphasis exists not to display Adams as a prude nor to display his naïveté in politics (he was not really so naïve),[33] but to emphasize that he must acknowledge his moral stance as the stance of an apologist for a faulty view of the world. This becomes clearest in "Darwinism" (15), in which, in a context of scientific speculation, he rejects the idea of history which somewhat alarmingly dawns upon him on Wenlock Edge precisely because it is based upon experimental concepts denying the idea of objective, absolute truth. "Henry Adams was the first in an infinite series to discover and admit to himself that he really did not care whether truth was, or was not, true" (15, pp. 231–32). Perhaps man organized his knowledge according to humanly created concepts. Perhaps eighteenth-century principles were not immutable. Perhaps even the science inspiring them was a genuine intellectual creation, and the harmony of the universe a human fabrication. In this case there was no objective truth. But the young moralist must remain an apologist for family and country, at least for the time being: "From the beginning of history, this attitude had been branded as criminal— worse than crime—sacrilege! Society punished it ferociously and justly in self-defence. Mr. Adams, the father, looked on it as moral weakness" (15, p. 232).

Whenever Adams plays the moralist, therefore, he is actually expressing the third tenet of his eighteenth-century world, a tenet which proscribes criticism of the validity of the first two propositions. Paradoxically, it is as moralist that he is most effective as an agent in his world, at least in the sense that, even if his action comes to naught, he is nonetheless capable of action. Moral motivations lead him

[33] In the "Declaration of Paris" Adams made clear that he was aware the British were guided by national self-interest.

to act upon Darwinist assumptions by returning to Washington after the Civil War as a vehement reformer wielding the pen as his sword. But there is another strand of his experiences through the chapter entitled "Failure" which, in conjunction with his obvious failure at reform, finally leads him to understand the limitations imposed upon knowledge by another fundamental premise of eighteenth-century education. All the while that as moralist he insists that America is unique and that it can express the harmony of nature, the Civil War notwithstanding, he is simultaneously led to question the value of the Lockean foundation of knowledge.

Earlier it was observed that Adams portrays the foundations of his eighteenth-century education as grounded in sensory data, so that the antinomies of the seasons suggested the fundamental problem of life:

From cradle to grave this problem of running order through chaos, direction through space, discipline through freedom, unity through multiplicity, has always been, and always must be, the task of education, as it is the moral of religion, philosophy, science, art, politics, and economy. [1, p. 12]

But if the senses presented the problem, could knowledge so grounded effect its solution? The second strand of Adams's experiences focuses upon sensory data to suggest that the senses cannot create any reliable human truths. Those experiences begin early, with his trip to Washington, which included a visit to his grandmother. The world of the South with its "May sunshine and shadow," its thick foliage and luxuriant smells was decidedly a friendly world, and the boy liked it. But the data of the senses were illusory, for this friendly world would soon be engaged in mortal combat with Quincy.

The young man soon broadens his education by learning of a conflict between the illusions of the senses and the events of history. One may take his stay in Rome as typical of the experiences of his first European journey (6). Everywhere the sensuous feelings generated by Rome somehow contradict the known facts of Rome's violent history, the collapse of Roman and medieval civilization. The illusions of the senses thus conflict with historical fact. Adams continues to be deceived for a time, but by the time he reaches "Chaos" (19) his sensory experiences culminate in a knowledge that sensory data are indeed deceptive and cannot be the foundation of reliable education. In contrast to the death of his sister are the mere illusions of nature; these are in radical opposition to the violence of his sister's death. He apprehends behind nature not a harmony of force but a destructive complexity of force: "For the first time, the stage-scenery of the senses collapsed" (20, p. 288). With his sister's death, then, Adams discovers that the senses conceal only chaos, and that they convey no certainties whatsoever—neither the certainties of an ordered universe which both science and society assumed nor the political corollaries derived from these certainties.

This second strand of experience—Adams's sensory education—is never far removed from the first, his education in morality; both converge upon the problem of American history. Throughout the first twenty chapters, Adams is caught in the dilemma posed by the Civil War, a dilemma which is ever present through references to its approach, through the knowledge of its actual occurrence, and through the events of its aftermath. And throughout he recognizes the threat to eighteenth-century principles which that war creates. Either the country's first principles are wrong, or man is simply immoral and a return to those principles can be achieved through vigorous human effort. As a moralist he hopes that the latter is true, but he is plagued by the doubts created by this second strand of experience. Those doubts are confirmed in the last part of the book, beginning with "Twenty Years After" (21), in which Adams finally affirms the need for a violent reconstruction of his eighteenth-century heritage, now exposed as theory rather than fact, and then proposes a new hypothesis.

Eighteenth-Century Assumptions and Twentieth-Century Revisions: Art as the Only Enduring Reality

Almost everywhere Adams looked during the course of his education, he saw paradox or confusion; and the record of it as set forth in the pages of the *Education* is filled with so many occurrences appearing strange and inexplicable to an eighteenth-century mind that to recount them all would be to duplicate the contents of the book. Although many of the paradoxes serve as obvious counterpoints to the world of the *Chartres,* these phenomena are symptoms rather than causes of the great changes taking place within the lifetime recorded in the *Education;* and, although it may be said that all the paradoxes are symptoms rather than causes, it is also true that some are more compelling than others, at least insofar as they effect a revolutionary change in the stultified eighteenth-century habits of thought which harass the persona and his world for so long. It is well to focus on these; they are only two, they subsume most of the minor paradoxes, and they lead directly to the transition from moralist to Conservative Christian Anarchist and scientific historian which represents the major change in the growth, and hence the education, of Henry Adams.

The first major paradox is the Civil War itself, for it denied the harmony of the natural world and spelled trouble for a political system presumed to effect a similar harmony in national life through the key concept of balance. Indeed, the failure to prevent the war, as well as the failure of human control in the diplomatic negotiations with England during the war (Charles Francis Adams's success, recall, is seen as providential), scuttled basic premises of eighteenth-century thought regarding the universe and

America itself. This has already been shown, and it has also been shown that the aftermath of the Civil War confirmed the implications of the war itself in Henry Adams's failure as reformer. America and the world at large, seen from the point of view of the eighteenth century, seemed to be dissolving into chaos rather than fulfilling the promise of its confident beginnings.

The second major paradox of the book is encountered by the persona in the last section, beginning with "Twenty Years After" (21). There the process of disintegration apparently becomes complete, for the advancement of a bankers' civilization finally destroys "the class into which Adams was born" (22, p. 345); but the process is attended by the curious phenomenon which is the reverse of chaos: consolidation. "In 1893, the issue came on the single gold standard, and the majority at last declared itself, once for all, in favor of the capitalistic system with all its necessary machinery." That system is a "mechanical consolidation of force," and it is "centralizing" (22, pp. 344, 345). In short, chaos gives way to a kind of unity unenvisioned by the eighteenth century, and this double vision of chaos and unity prevails throughout the remaining pages of the book. Ultimately the question becomes, "How explain change?"

To put the issue in these terms is to run the risk of reducing the *Education* to the level of triteness; but a moment's reflection will show that, within the historic situation defined by the book, the phrasing is perfectly appropriate and, to an eighteenth-century mind, cosmically shocking. The eighteenth-century world had overthrown the past in the name of truth based on science. In this sense it had effected an end to history conceived of as significant change. Having discovered eternal and immutable principles, the world could only grow better, and the religious aura which is spread over the early pages of the *Education* in the name of Enlightenment concepts shows how unshakable a faith it was: "What had been would continue to be" (1, p. 16).

The discovery that it *was* a faith, the awareness that the same fate had overtaken the eighteenth century which overtook the thirteenth, shakes the narrator into a historic, as opposed to the ahistoric, point of view. If Quincy could die, then history itself was eternal change ending in death, and the narrator could justly say of his persona, who by chapter 22 is rapidly approaching him in age and breadth of view, "After this vigorous impulse, nothing remained for a historian but to ask—how long and how far!" (p. 345).

This recognition is the final shock of Adams's education, if that education is conceived negatively as a stripping away of old illusions. It comes in Washington, shortly after he has viewed the Chicago Exposition, and is therefore intimately connected with the problem of American history. A capitalist America could never be an eighteenth-century America, nor could the fact of such a change possibly be explained in terms of older conceptions of the country. What follows this recognition is consistent with the implications of this shock. As Conservative Christian Anarchist, Henry Adams consciously acknowledges that all the principles which had commanded his allegiance were illusions— and untenable ones because they created a framework for viewing experience which darkened rather than lighted his way in a new world. Seeing history as eternal change, and America as part of the process, he seeks to give this new philosophy substantive form by devising a practicable theory for understanding history consonant with the precepts of his new views.

The logic of his turning to science to formulate a theory is clear. In a world of analogous planes of existence, where harmony in one sphere pointed to harmony in another, the rise of a new unity defying the political and social assumptions of eighteenth-century America necessarily questioned the stability of the Newtonian universe which imparted a glow of optimism to eighteenth-century thought. Hence Henry Adams, despite the knowledge that "all his associates in history condemned such an attempt as futile and almost immoral," returned to "the starting point of Sir Isaac Newton" (34, pp. 376–77). Of course, he was looking for a scientific law of history, but the values of the search were in their philosophical implications rather than in the tentative findings, particularly as the search is presented in the *Education*.

William Jordy has confirmed Adams's interest in the philosophical implications of science.[34] When Henry Adams turned to science, he was attracted to phenomenalists like Ernst Mach, Henri Poincaré, and Karl Pearson (whose book, *The Grammar of Science,* became the title of chapter 31 in the *Education*). Not interested in the details of science, but in its "mass" (24, p. 377), he comprehended that mass to his own satisfaction by studying the work of men who insisted that scientific constructs, even those of Newton, were hypotheses which may or may not correspond to reality, but whose whole value lay in explaining phenomena coherently. Science rejected old hypotheses when new phenomena defied an established scientific view, and contrived new ones to remove the paradoxes created by new observations and to generate further research.

Given this hypothetical nature of science, Adams utilized the same method for writing history in the *Chartres* and the *Education*. He turned away from the Rankean method of his earlier *History,* which smacked too much of Newton in its insistence upon collecting the facts and letting generalizations arise in the mind of a passive reader and historian. Instead he adopted the relativism of these late works which led to hypotheses derived from science to remove the paradoxes of experience which he encountered in American life. The formulas based on a faith in Newton had

[34] See Jordy's chapter 7, "The Limit of Thought," especially pp. 227–42. Jordy takes Adams to task for his belief that the new science would lead to chaos. Rather than seeing him as the philosopher of history, Jordy's book concentrates on the literal aspects of the essays and not on the broader logic of the *Education*.

failed. The second law of thermodynamics provided a surer foundation, at least in the sense that it explained paradox.

Insofar as Adams's hypothesis was intended to generate further research into bringing history in line with the sciences, his appeal can only be to the antiquarian, who catalogs the curiosities of past ambitions doomed to failure before they start. But in the *Education,* Adams was less interested in asserting than asking; and though his artistic structure does assert, it affirms only as art affirms, and the questions come through clearly nonetheless. The questions he saw science raising, rather than the hypothetical answers he offered, are the measure of the man's greatness.

The first question was undeniably modern. How can man live in a world where all areas of the universe do not cohere? Critics are fond of saying that Adams was medieval in this desire, or grasping tenaciously his Puritan inheritance,[35] but such judgments obscure the source of such a view—a science which transcended a Puritan heritage to dominate the eighteenth century and, in the form of Darwinism, to affect the nineteenth century as well. Seen in the light of science's influence, therefore, the assumption of a correspondence between the human and the nonhuman world is not so remote from contemporary experience as it might appear on the surface.

Applied to the *Education,* such comments violate the primary message of the book, its greatest challenge, that for the first time and henceforth in the history of man such correspondences cannot be assumed as true, simply because science, the modern source of man's knowledge of reality, has grown too frankly hypothetical in its statements to allow man to enter into a relation with reality. It seems curious, of course, that the author of a book with this point of view would, in his essays, hypothesize along

---

[35] Yvor Winters began this trend of criticism in his *The Anatomy of Nonsense.* Jordy calls Adams medieval in his methods in writing the "Letter," p. 214.

lines suggesting the opposite: that indeed there is a harmony existing in several spheres of the universe, even though it is the harmony of decay. But the contradiction is more apparent than real, after all, unless one separates the essays from the *Education* and thus stresses Adams's literal scientific goal: to discover a single law governing man and nature. Man may not be able to do this, but the *Education* insists that he must establish *some* meaningful relationship with science. Implicit in the book is a second question: How can philosophy, a study of reality, accommodate itself to the new face of science?

Always more the philosopher than the scientific historian, Adams knew that Western philosophy had perennially adjusted to scientific views of reality. No matter how unscientific the Aristotelian physics of Saint Thomas might appear to moderns, it became the basis for Aquinas's proof of God. Just as surely as Aquinas used Aristotle, Locke adapted his theory of ideas to the physics of Newton. And, despite the complexity of modern science, contemporary man would have to devise a philosophy accordingly. If those precepts of science presumed a purely hypothetical world, subject to incredibly rapid change, his philosophy must take such elements into account. To the extent that philosophy's appointed task of bringing man into relation with science must continue, to that extent the mind must also continue to discover harmony in several spheres—though with this fundamental difference: that such harmony now must be acknowledged as clearly a human fabrication, not of God's making nor inherent in nature. And if man could succeed in this task, the framework of new ideas and values required by a generation might be established.

The third question science raised harked back to a more familiar problem: the value of the senses. In the last part of the *Education,* with its numerous dichotomies between art and the shapeless present, Adams discovers that value when he encounters the world of science. Karl Pearson's famous image of the telephone exchange to define the relationship of mind to external phenomena impressed Adams. As Jordy describes the meaning of that image, "the mind was a unique kind of exchange in which the operator was forever locked so that he never got closer to his subscribers than the network of wires intervening between his switchboard and their instruments."[36] Thus bound by his senses, separated forever from reality, Adams could write in his personal copy of *The Grammar of Science:* "If the universe to us exists only as sense-impressions, surely this merely turns the universe into us, as a part or the whole of us."[37] To Henry Adams, science seemed to have destroyed its old assumption of a bifurcation of reality between the mental substance, man, and the material objects composing the world—a reality in which man, through his science, could transcend his subjective view of the outside world, and know it as it really existed in a public world of space and time which was true, not subjective, reality. On that scientific assumption of a division between the human and the material world Locke created his theory of ideas, specifying a world composed of mental substances and material objects, and ideas arising from their interaction; but now science itself seemed to pull the rug out from under Locke's feet just as Berkeley did when he demonstrated that if the mind knows only sense data, the physical world becomes a function of mind; and just as Hume did when, going one step further, he reduced the mind itself to a meaningless collection of sense data.[38] Truly, Adams could write of the

[36] Jordy, pp. 233–34.

[37] Quoted by Jordy, p. 235.

[38] Northrop treats extensively the Newtonian insistence upon a public world of space and time, as opposed to the subjective world of Lockean secondary qualities, a division which would presuppose a bifurcation of reality, as Locke thought. See pp. 75–79. He treats Berkeley and Hume as pointing out important contradictions in Locke's theory of ideas. Unlike Henry Adams, however, he does not see modern trends in science as destroying the conception of the existence of a public realm of space and time (see p. 76). It was this assumption, probably an incorrect one, which led Adams to his ultimate pessimism.

new science: "Philosophy has never got beyond this point. There are but two schools; one turns the world onto me; the other turns me onto the world; and the result is the same."[39] That result was a world in which no first principles could ever be appealed to as absolute and true in themselves.

But the result gave added status and dignity to what Adams earlier termed "education only sensual." The prestige of art necessarily soared. Although art and science are in one respect equivalent, since each organizes sense data in its own way, the work of art never attempts to transcend the senses. It deals with the only things all men know, sense data, and it gives those data form; as such it is a concrete, real, nonhypothetical expression of man's own felt need for unity, and it is an immediate realization of that unity, unlike a science which hypothesizes a partial world known only through nonsensuous abstractions.

Rightly or wrongly, with this conviction that science had destroyed a world knowable as reality, not hypothesis, Henry Adams, the man of science, was transformed into the artist. Although he pretended to a scientific method in his essays, at least insofar as he created hypotheses to explain paradoxes, he showed that these speculations were part of his private world; it was, after all, in the form of art, not of science or history, that he presented a dynamic theory of history to a reading public. If it does possess validity, if it does extend beyond his own personal experience, it is because art always so extends and communicates, and its truths challenge the theories of the scientist and the facts of the historian. It is as art that we must view the version of history affirmed by the inseparable unit: *Mont-Saint-Michel and Chartres* and *The Education of Henry Adams*. Not as history, not as science, but as art can the reader appreciate the novel thesis that the Civil

[39] Letter of 13 May 1905, Ford, 2: 451.

War was the result of the dispute between nominalism and realism whose champions, Pierre du Pallet, called Peter Abelard, and Guillaume de Champeaux, debated many centuries before the earth was proved round and America discovered.

History as Metaphor: The *Chartres* and the *Education* as a Unit

The analysis of the *Chartres* in chapter 1 distinguished three purposes for Adams's subjective method. Through it Adams elevated his persona into a collective Western consciousness, created aesthetic generalizations through a carefully controlled method of association, and made his persona's subjective responses the "constant" in a "scientific" experiment designed to measure the relative powers of two symbols, Virgin and dynamo. This last use of subjectivity for scientific purposes is of special relevance here because it points to the philosophy of history held by the Conservative Christian Anarchist and links the modern world with the past. At first sight it would appear that a subjective approach to both worlds is folly. The Virgin's force, conceived of as objectively real by medieval man, had its wellspring in instinct, the force of sex. In that sense the medieval world was subjective, and from such subjectivity the modern world sought escape by positing its values in reason and directing its attention to the physical universe. Instinct thus surrendered to reason, and a subjective world yielded to the objective world of science. Henry Adams certainly agreed that instinct had lost its hold in the centuries intervening between Saint Francis of Assisi and John Quincy Adams; but the world, although it thought otherwise, had not become less subjective. To Adams, man's science, like medieval theology, had failed to correspond to reality; and indeed the Conservative Christian Anarchist finally concluded that all formulations of reality—whether scientific, religious, or philosophical—were genuine human creations. In this sense the world created by reason was as subjective as that created by instinct; both worlds were human projections imposed on a supposed "reality" which had neither meaning nor form independent of man.

Upon this assertion of the impossibility of escape from the self, Henry Adams insisted upon constructing a formula for history, impatiently declaring his right to do so. But how avoid whimsy or sheer arbitrariness? And has Adams avoided these? Clearly his theory of history was never offered as an impromptu alternative to standard views of history, but was proffered as the solution to problems which had arisen through the maintenance of a traditional, eighteenth-century mentality. Precisely because they were many in number and staggering in significance, he could try a new adventure in education designed to integrate exceptions to older beliefs within a new conceptual framework. It has been shown that, for him, these problems converged on traditional notions of American history. Now it remains only to see how this theory of history unites his masterpieces to remove those problems and provides a new understanding of history.

The fundamental assumption of the eighteenth-century American was that his country was unique, representing a sharp, clean break with the past and possessing a happy future consistent with the principles of its founding. But national change following the Civil War—the rise of corruption and the trend toward internationalism in the later part of the century—convinced Henry Adams that America had to be restored to history. It had not broken with the past, nor was its future to be any different from the world's. If it represented the avant-garde in the family of nations, it was only because it displayed in bolder relief those lines of development, unforeseen and undesired by the eighteenth century, which the rest of the world was soon to exhibit. Thus the artistry of the *Chartres-Education* unit focuses upon the American past and the American future to correct the erroneous assumption of America's uniqueness and to remove the paradoxes of American history generated by this idea.

In exact opposition to eighteenth-century tenets, the *Chartres-Education* unit insists that, rather than complete divorcement from the medieval past, American history began as a disintegration of the synthesis of medieval life. The subjective moments of the persona in the *Education* disclose this disintegration on a personal level. Henry Adams is forever attracted to the medieval world, and he is forever pulled back by the strictures of his eighteenth-century inheritance. The elements of his personality are in obvious competition, and the competition which on his first European journey assumes historical proportions is earlier foreshadowed by the rival attractions exerted by Quincy and the South. But the persona, recall, is a microcosm of the competing factions within the nation at large, and the portrayal of these factions links the world of the *Education* with that of the *Chartres*.

Balance is proclaimed as a virtue in the early education of Adams because it is presumed to reproduce the harmony prevailing in the natural world; but the structure of the narrative places this conception in ironic variance with the developments in American life. Rather than representing a unique departure from the past, the opening three chapters display a nation in which a tentative sectional balance can be seen as the breakup of medieval synthesis. Act, intuition, and reason were synthesized by the controlling element, intuition, within the Transition portrayed by the *Chartres*. Now reason has come to the fore, in the symbol of Quincy, and it seeks not to synthesize but to balance the South and Boston. The South is the world of act and emotion totally divorced from reason; Boston represents the mechanical force of science which, since the time of Francis Bacon, has been making headway and intruding itself into the medie-

val equilibrium. To both of these forces Quincy, portrayed
as a degraded relic of a religious phase of existence, is hostile; and to both, it must play the role of mediator. The
Civil War shows that failure concretely, but within the light
of the *Chartres,* it is more than a failure of the Adamses,
even more than a failure of eighteenth-century notions of
a harmonious universe. It is the failure of the medieval synthesis itself. For centuries that synthesis has been dissolving under the impact of forces released through scientific
method. In the early pages of the *Education* it reaches its
critical point, and then the explosion, as society passes into
a new phase, the mechanical. The Civil War is the breakup
of the Transition!

Thus the world of the *Education* destroys both Mont-
Saint-Michel and Chartres, and that destruction—not ironically at all—is effected by the same kind of violent military action which created it. Behind the symbolism of Saint
Michael lay a world of military energy asserting the unity
of one God rather than the multiplicity of pagan gods still
worshiped by tenth-century Normans. Even if unity was
an illusory ideal, man insisted upon it. As Henry Adams of
the *Education* wrote, "Apparently one never denied it" (29,
p. 432). The eighteenth century did not deny it; by de-
throning revelation and placing scientific laws in its stead,
it preserved the effects of unity. Yet within that world, portrayed by the *Education,* all the old values attached to the
forces of medieval life have been completely inverted as
well as fractured. For the military energies that erected
Mont-Saint-Michel now serve the cause of a South whose
degraded emotionalism seeks to destroy a unity which, at
its medieval height, it had effected. And Quincy, the repository of reason, has replaced the energy of Chartres, which
by intuition sought synthesis, whereas its historic successor
sought merely balance. Hence within the holocaust of war
both Quincy and the South are destroyed, for their reversal
of traditional values implies their weakened power as forces,

and the newer force of mechanical Boston gains by default. The effects of this victory automatically deny the second assumption of American history: that its future should be distinctive, just as its past was unique. Instead of a highly individual nation, the pages of the *Education* portray an America whose Civil War is merely a local image of forces contending within all of civilization and inexorably directing the movement of man's thought toward a supersensual nominalist world whose reality could never be known. The nominalist, Abelard, had come into his own at last. The defeat of William of Champeaux, advocate of realism, was permanent.

The forces affecting American life were first displayed through a controlled use of subjectivity in the *Chartres*. Through a controlled system of equivalences and correspondences, these forces reappeared in the *Education,* where Adams's artistry is consummated at a high level. The book is successful because, as art, it achieves the difficult goal Henry Adams set out for himself:

He used to say, half in jest, that his great ambition was to complete St. Augustine's "Confessions," but that St. Augustine, like a great artist, had worked from multiplicity to unity, while he, like a small one, had to reverse the method and work back from unity to multiplicity. [1918 preface, vii–viii]

This prefatory aside need not have been self-depreciating, for the *Education* does complete the *Confessions,* and its literary success is consistent with Adams's desire to display that movement of thought in history which he hoped could later be charted by science. The progress of the *Education* is a movement from an eighteenth-century Quincy where Henry Adams's grandfather had sat in his pew "since the time of St. Augustine" (1, p. 15) to the climactic discovery of radium when the thread of history, its assumption of unity in several spheres of the universe, and hence its "continuity[,] snapped" (31, p. 457). Seen as a movement away from an ordered universe, where the harmony of Augustine's Christian God is now defined through the harmony of Newton's laws, the *Education* picks up where Augustine's *Confessions* leaves off. God's mystery has yielded to the less mystical harmonies of science, but harmony still prevails until the advent of new forces and a new science seriously jeopardizes, if not destroys, the possibilities for its twentieth-century re-creation. If the idea of such a movement in man's thought now seems a commonplace, and Adam's literal desire for unity a historical curiosity, his art remains to vindicate both. "He was morbidly curious to see some light at the end of the passage" (26, p. 396), Adams recorded in his *Education*. As an artist, he cast quite as much light as he saw.

Works Cited

Adams, Brooks. *Law of Civilization and Decay.* New York: Alfred A. Knopf, 1943.

Adams, Henry. *Chapters of Erie and Other Essays.* (In collaboration with Charles F. Adams, Jr.) Boston: James R. Osgood and Co., 1871.

———. *The Degradation of the Democratic Dogma,* with an introduction by Brooks Adams. (Includes: "The Tendency of History," 1894; "The Rule of Phase Applied to History," 1909; and "A Letter to American Teachers of History," 1910). New York: The Macmillan Co., 1919.

———. *Democracy: An American Novel.* New York: Henry Holt and Co., Inc., 1880.

———. *The Education of Henry Adams: An Autobiography.* Boston and New York: Houghton Mifflin Co., 1918.

———. *Esther, a Novel,* by Francis Snow Compton. New York: Houghton Mifflin Co., 1884.

———. *Henry Adams and His Friends. A Collection of His Unpublished Letters,* compiled with a biographical introduction by Harold Dean Cater. Boston: Houghton Mifflin Co., 1947.

———. *Historical Essays.* New York: Charles Scribner's Sons, 1891.

———. *History of the United States of America during the Administrations of Thomas Jefferson and James Madison.* 9 vols. New York: Charles Scribner's Sons, 1889–91.

———. *John Randolph.* Boston and New York: Houghton Mifflin Co., 1882.

————. *Letters of Henry Adams,* ed. Worthington Chauncey Ford, 2 vols. (1858–91 and 1892–1918). Boston and New York: Houghton Mifflin Co., 1930 and 1938.

————. *Life of Albert Gallatin.* Philadelphia: J. B. Lippincott Co., 1879.

————. *Life of George Cabot Lodge.* Boston and New York: Houghton Mifflin Co., 1911.

————. *Mont-Saint-Michel and Chartres.* Boston and New York: Houghton Mifflin Co., 1933.

Adams, John Quincy. "An Oration Addressed to the Citizens of the Town of Quincy on the Fourth of July, 1831, the Fifty Fifth Anniversary of the Independence of the United States of America," *Slavery Pamphlets.* Vol. 22. Boston: Richardson, Lord, and Holbrook, 1831.

Baym, Max I. *The French Education of Henry Adams.* New York: Columbia University Press, 1951.

Becker, Carl L. *The Declaration of Independence: A Study in the History of Political Ideas.* New York, 1940.

————. "The Education of Henry Adams." *American Historical Review* 24 (April 1919): 422–34.

————. *Every Man His Own Historian.* New York, 1935.

————. Review of *The Degradation of the Democratic Dogma. American Historial Review,* 25 (1920): 480–82.

Beringause, Arthur F. *Brooks Adams: A Biography.* New York: Alfred A. Knopf, 1955.

Blackmur, R. P. "Adams Goes to School: I. The Problem Laid Out." *Kenyon Review* 46 (1955): 597–623.

————. "The Expense of Greatness: Three Emphases on Henry Adams." *Virginia Quarterly Review* 12 (July 1936): 396–415.

————. "Harmony of True Liberalism: Henry Adams's *Mont-Saint-Michel and Chartres.*" *Sewanee Review* 60 (1952): 1–27.

————. "The Novels of Henry Adams." *Sewanee Review* 51 (1943): 281–304.

————. "The Virgin and the Dynamo." *Magazine of Art* 45 (April 1952): 147–53.

Blunt, Reverend H. F., "The Maleducation of Henry Adams." *Catholic World* 145 (April 1937): 46–52.

Braun, Hugh, *Historical Architecture: The Development of Structure and Design.* New York: Thomas Yoseloff, 1959.

Cairns, John C. "The Successful Quest of Henry Adams."
  South Atlantic Quarterly 57 (Spring 1958): 168–93.
Cargill, Oscar. "The Medievalism of Henry Adams." in *Essays
  and Studies in Honor of Carleton Brown.* New York, 1940,
  pp. 296–324.
Dictionary of American Biography. New York, 1931.
Donald, David. *Charles Sumner and the Coming of the Civil
  War.* New York, 1960.
Donovan, Timothy Paul. *Henry Adams and Brooks Adams: The
  Education of Two American Historians.* Norman: University
  of Oklahoma Press, 1961.
Healy, Sister Mary Aquinas. "A Study of Non-Rational
  Elements in the Works of Henry Adams as Centralized in His
  Attitude toward Women." *Dissertation Abstracts* 16 (1956):
  2163. Dissertation at the University of Wisconsin, 1956.
Hochfield, George. *Henry Adams: An Introduction and
  Interpretation.* American Authors and Critics Series. New
  York: Barnes and Noble, Inc., 1962.
Hume, Robert A. *Runaway Star: An Appreciation of Henry
  Adams.* Ithaca, New York: Cornell University Press, 1951.
Jordy, William. *Henry Adams, Scientific Historian.* New Haven:
  Yale University Press, 1952.
Kariel, Henry S. "The Limits of Social Science: Henry Adams's
  Quest for Order." *American Political Science Review* 50
  (1956): 1074–92.
Laslett, Peter, ed. Introduction to John Locke's *Two Treatises of
  Government.* Cambridge: At the University Press, 1960.
Levenson, J. C. *The Mind and Art of Henry Adams.* Boston:
  Houghton Mifflin Co., 1957.
Lipsky, George. *John Quincy Adams, His Theory and Ideas.*
  New York, 1950.
Locke, John. *Essay concerning Human Understanding.*
Lyon, Melvin Earnest. "Symbol and Idea in the Major Works of
  Henry Adams." *Dissertation Abstracts* 21: 623–24.
  Dissertation at the University of Wisconsin, 1960.
MacLean, Kenneth. "Window and Cross in Henry Adams's
  Education." *University of Toronto Quarterly* 28 (July 1959):
  332–44.
Munford, Howard M. "Henry Adams and the Tendency of
  History." *New England Quarterly* 32 (March 1959): 79–90.

———. "Henry Adams: The Limitations of Science." *Southern Review* 4 (1968): n.s. 59–71.

Newton, Sir Isaac. *Mathematical Principles of Natural Philosophy.*

Northrop, F. S. C. *The Meeting of East and West: An Inquiry concerning World Understanding.* New York, 1946.

Pope, Alexander. *Essay on Criticism.*

———. *Essay on Man.*

Quinlivan, Frances. "Irregularities of the Mental Mirror." *Catholic World* 163 (April 1946): 58–65.

Runes, Dagobert D. *Dictionary of Philosophy.* New York, 1942.

Samuels, Ernest. *The Young Henry Adams.* Cambridge, Mass.: Harvard University Press, 1948.

———. *Henry Adams: The Middle Years.* Cambridge, Mass.: Harvard University Press, 1958.

———. *Henry Adams: The Major Phase.* Cambridge, Mass.: Harvard University Press, 1964.

Stevenson, Elizabeth. *Henry Adams: A Biography.* New York: The Macmillan Co., 1956.

Taylor, Henry Osborn. Review of *Mont-Saint-Michel and Chartres. American Historical Review* 19 (April 1914): 592–94.

Van Zandt, Roland. *The Metaphysical Foundations of American History.* The Hague: Mouton and Co., 1959.

Walcutt, Charles Child. *American Literary Naturalism: A Divided Stream.* Minneapolis: University of Minnesota Press, 1956.

Welland, D. S. R. "Henry Adams as Novelist." *Renaissance and Modern Studies* (University of Nottingham) 3 (1959): 25–50.

White, Lynn, Jr., "Dynamo and Virgin Reconsidered." *American Scholar* 27 (Spring 1958): 183–94.

Whitehead, Alfred North. *Science and the Modern World.* New York, 1941.

Winters, Yvor. "Henry Adams; or, The Creation of Confusion." In *The Anatomy of Nonsense.* Norfolk, Conn.: New Directions, 1943; reprinted in *In Defense of Reason.* New York: William Morrow and Co., 1947.

Wright, Nathalia. "Henry Adams's Theory of History: A Puritan Defense." *New England Quarterly* 58 (1945): 204–10.

Index